ESTABLISHING YOUR GOALS

CAMBRIDGE ADULT EDUCATION
A Division of Simon & Schuster
Upper Saddle River, New Jersey

Executive Editor: Mark Moscowitz
Project Editors: Laura Baselice, Lynn W. Kloss, Robert McIlwaine
Writer: Theresa Flynn-Nason
Production Manager: Penny Gibson
Production Editor: Nicole Cypher
Marketing Manager: Will Jarred
Interior Electronic Design: Mimi Raihl
Illustrator: Allen Davis
Photo Research: Jenifer Hixon
Electronic Page Production: Mimi Raihl
Cover Design: Mimi Raihl

Printed in the United States of America.
1 2 3 4 5 6 7 8 9 10 99 98 97 96 95
ISBN: 0-8359-4673-8

Cambridge Adult Education
A Division of Simon & Schuster
Upper Saddle River, New Jersey

Contents

UNIT 1: THE IMPORTANCE OF SELF-ESTEEM   **1**

    Lesson 1: What Is Self-Esteem?   3

    Lesson 2: Goals and Self-Esteem   7

    Lesson 3: Improve Your Self-Esteem   11

    Unit 1 Review   15

UNIT 2: STRENGTHS AND WEAKNESSES   **17**

    Lesson 4: Be Positive   19

    Lesson 5: Identify Your Strengths and Weaknesses   23

    Lesson 6: Concentrate on Your Strengths   25

    Unit 2 Review   28

Real-World Connection: The Neat Freak   **30**

Unit 3: VALUES   **34**

    Lesson 7: Right and Wrong   36

    Lesson 8: Know Your Values   40

    Lesson 9: Goals and Values   43

    Unit 3 Review   46

Real-World Connection: The Letter   **48**

UNIT 4:   **GOALS**   **52**

Lesson 10:   Set Goals   55

Lesson 11:   Set Goals: Your Turn   62

Unit 4 Review   64

UNIT 5:   **BELONGING**   **66**

Lesson 12:   The Importance of Belonging   68

Lesson 13:   Finding the Right Group   73

Lesson 14:   Dealing With Peer Pressure   77

Unit 5 Review   82

UNIT 6:   **RESPECT DIFFERENCES**   **84**

Lesson 15:   Discrimination   86

Lesson 16:   Show Respect for Others   91

Unit 6 Review   96

UNIT 7:   **PUT IT INTO PRACTICE**   **98**

Reviewing Unit 1: The Importance of Self-Esteem   99

Reviewing Unit 2: Strengths and Weaknesses   101

Reviewing Unit 3: Values   103

Reviewing Unit 4: Goals   105

Reviewing Unit 5: Belonging   108

Reviewing Unit 6: Respect Differences   110

BOOK REVIEW   **112**

GLOSSARY   **115**

ANSWER KEY   **116**

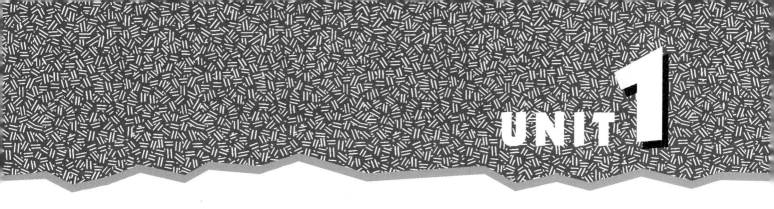

The Importance of Self-Esteem

In this unit you will:

- learn about self-esteem.
- discover that high self-esteem helps you work toward your goals.
- explore ways of improving self-esteem.

Key Words

self-esteem: your opinion of yourself
goal: something you hope to achieve
positive: good; healthy
negative: bad; harmful

Meet Jack Carter

Jack Carter has just lost his job. He used to work at a nursing home. He worked in the laundry room.

Jack really liked the job. He didn't mind walking all over the building to pick up the dirty laundry. It gave him a chance to talk with the people who lived there. They all seemed to know Jack's route. Many of the old people would wait by their doors for him to pass. They would stop Jack. They would tell him about their day.

Jack always took the time to listen to their stories. He would pay attention to them. He would give them a friendly smile. Jack knew that a few dirty clothes could wait. He knew that it was important to be kind to lonely people.

But Jack's boss did not feel the same way. He told Jack that his job was picking up laundry, not talking to old people.

Think About It

Circle the letter of the statement that *best* completes each sentence. (Check your answers on page 116.)

1. Jack used to work in a
   a. cleaner's.
   b. nursing home.
   c. restaurant.
   d. hospital.

2. Jack thinks that it is important to
   a. listen to others.
   b. work quickly.
   c. avoid old people.
   d. ignore the boss.

What Is Self-Esteem?

One day, Jack Carter's boss asked Jack to come into his office. He shut the door.

"Jack," he began. "I have some bad news. I'm afraid I'm going to have to let you go."

Jack was surprised. "Why?" he asked.

"I'm afraid you aren't doing a good job," his boss replied.

"What do you mean?" Jack said. "I'm one of the best workers in the laundry room."

"Yes, when you're in the laundry room you're a great worker," his boss said. "But the problem is you're not in the laundry room as much as you should be. You spend too much time out of the laundry room."

"You mean talking to the people who live here," Jack answered. "I know that's not part of my job. But I cannot just walk away from a person who is talking to me. I think that's very rude."

"Well, rude or not, it wastes too much time. I need someone in the laundry room. I need someone taking care of the dirty clothes."

The boss stood up. "I'm sorry, Jack. My secretary will give you your last paycheck."

Jack stood. He slowly walked toward the door. "Jack," the boss called after him. "I'll keep you in mind for other jobs that might become available here. You have a good way with people. The residents like your company. You would make a great aide. Part of that job is talking with the people who live here. If I hear of any aide openings, I'll call you."

Circle the letter of the best answer to the question.
(Check your answer on page 116.)

What did the boss want to tell Jack?

   a. Jack is getting a raise.

   b. Jack is doing a good job.

   c. Jack is fired.

   d. The people who live in the nursing home don't like Jack.

The Meaning of Self-Esteem

When Jack left his boss's office, he was disappointed. He felt bad about losing his job. He knew that he had gotten his last paycheck. He was worried about paying his bills.

But Jack did not feel bad about himself. Why? Jack knows that he is a valuable person. He knows that he is good at some things. He knows that he is not so good at other things.

Jack's boss also knows that Jack is good at some things. Jack's boss said that Jack "had a way with the elderly." This is a special skill. Not everyone has this skill. But Jack does!

Jack understands why he lost the job. He wasn't suited for the laundry room. That job called for skills that Jack didn't have. To be good at that job, Jack would have had to ignore the old people. To be good at that job, Jack would have had to think about things rather than people. Jack couldn't do that.

How can Jack feel good about himself even after losing his job? Jack has high self-esteem. **Self-esteem** is your opinion of yourself. People with high self-esteem value themselves. They know that they are good at some things. They know that they are not so good at other things. They are comfortable with themselves. They like themselves. They understand themselves.

Think About It

Imagine that you are a friend of Jack. You just received a letter from him. In the letter, Jack tells you about losing his job. He explains why the boss let him go. In the space provided, write a letter to Jack. Be sure to give your friend some advice about what he should do now.

Dear Jack,

What About You?

Read each statement. Circle the number that *best* describes *you* most of the time.

1. I know that I am good at certain things.

5	4	3	2	1
Always		Sometimes		Never

2. I feel good about myself.

5	4	3	2	1
Always		Sometimes		Never

3. I accept the fact that I make mistakes.

5	4	3	2	1
Always		Sometimes		Never

4. I know that I am not perfect.

5	4	3	2	1
Always		Sometimes		Never

5. I am proud to be me.

5	4	3	2	1
Always		Sometimes		Never

6. I feel that I have the right to be happy.

5	4	3	2	1
Always		Sometimes		Never

7. I feel that I have some control over my life.

5	4	3	2	1
Always		Sometimes		Never

Look over the previous page.

- Did you circle 4 or 5 for any statements? These ratings show high self-esteem.

- Did you circle 1 or 2 for any statements? These ratings show low self-esteem.

- Did you circle 3 for any statement? This rating shows that you could work on your self-esteem.

- Review your ratings. In the space provided, describe the areas in which you show high self-esteem. Then name the areas in which you need to work on your self-esteem.

High Self-Esteem

Low Self-Esteem

Check What You've Learned _____

Read each statement. If the statement is true, write T on the answer blank. If the statement is false, write F on the answer blank. (Check your answers on page 116.)

_____ 1. Self-esteem is the way other people feel about you.

_____ 2. People with high self-esteem are good at everything.

_____ 3. People with high self-esteem like themselves.

_____ 4. High self-esteem means valuing yourself.

_____ 5. People with high self-esteem make mistakes.

Goals and Self-Esteem

Every person has an opinion of himself or herself. Some people think highly of themselves. These people have high self-esteem. Some people have a low opinion of themselves. These people have low self-esteem.

Self-esteem is a personal thing. It is your feeling about *you!*

Self-esteem does not come from other people. It comes from deep inside you.

Remember Jack Carter? He was fired from his job. But Jack did not let losing his job change his opinion about himself. He still liked himself, even though he no longer had a job. This is because Jack had high self-esteem. His opinion of himself came from his thoughts and feelings. Jack did not let losing his job change his opinion of himself. He knew that he was valuable.

Trying New Things

Self-esteem affects many of the things you do. If you have high self-esteem, you think favorably about yourself. You believe that you are valuable. You know that you are good at certain things.

High self-esteem helps you try new things. How? If you have high self-esteem, you are confident about yourself. You are willing to try new things. You believe that you have a chance to succeed.

Low self-esteem keeps you from trying new things. People with low self-esteem don't feel valuable. They think that they aren't good at anything. They are scared to try new things. Why? People with low self-esteem think that they will probably fail. They assume the worst.

What About You?

Think about the last time someone asked you to do something that you had never done before. Answer these questions about the experience. Write the answers in the space provided.

1. What were you asked to do?

2. Did you try it? Or did you refuse to try?

3. Why did you act this way?

4. If you did try something new, how did it work out? Were you successful? Or did you fail?

5. Think about what you have learned about self-esteem. What do your actions show about *your* self-esteem? Did your actions show that you believe in yourself? Or did your actions show that you thought that you would fail?

Personal Goals

Everybody has goals. A **goal** is something you hope to achieve. It is something you work toward.

Goals are personal things. Not all people hope to achieve exactly the same thing. People are different. Their goals are different.

You have your own goals. Right now, you are working through this book. Why? You must have a certain goal in mind. Perhaps your goal is to learn something new. Perhaps your goal is to understand yourself a little better. Perhaps your goal is to improve yourself.

What About You?

You are working through this book to achieve some goal. Write your goal in the space provided.

Self-Esteem Helps!

Your self-esteem can help you to reach your goals. Or it may stop you from achieving what you want to achieve. How? High self-esteem gives you a feeling of power. It helps keep you strong. High self-esteem helps you work toward your goals.

Low self-esteem keeps you from reaching your goals. Low self-esteem gives you a feeling of hopelessness. If you have low self-esteem, you feel as though everything you do is wrong. People with low self-esteem don't even try to reach their goals. They feel as if it's not worth the effort. They think that they will just fail!

What About You?

1. Listed below are some common goals. Put a check mark next to the goals that you hope to achieve.

_____ I want to have a good life.

_____ I want to be happy.

_____ I want to be a good parent.

_____ I want to be a good partner.

_____ I want to learn more.

_____ I want to live in a nice place.

_____ I want to be physically fit.

_____ I want to be kind to others.

_____ I want to be a good worker.

_____ I want to stop my bad habits.

_____ I want to have a healthy body.

_____ I want to save more money.

_____ I want to be a good friend.

2. Do you have any goals that are not listed above? Write them in the space provided.

3. Look over the list of goals on the previous page. Choose one goal that you checked. Explain how you are working toward that goal.

Check What You've Learned

Read each statement. If the statement is true, write T on the answer blank. If the statement is false, write F on the answer blank. (Check your answers on page 116.).

_____ **1.** Self-esteem comes from other people's opinions of you.

_____ **2.** People with low self-esteem like to try new things.

_____ **3.** High self-esteem gives you a feeling of power.

_____ **4.** All people have the same goals.

_____ **5.** Low self-esteem helps you reach your goals.

Improve Your Self-Esteem

You have learned that high self-esteem can help you reach your goals. But what if you lack high self-esteem? Does this mean that you will never reach your goals? Absolutely not! You can change your self-esteem. With a little hard work, you can change low self-esteem into high self-esteem.

Take a Good Look at the Positive

In order to change self-esteem, you need to think about yourself. You must think about who you are and what you do. You have to take some time to really get to know you!

First, think about the things that you do well. Everyone has **positive**, or good, points. Think about yours.

What About You?

Listed below are some positive traits. Put a check mark next to the traits that you possess.

_____ I'm a good worker.   _____ I'm a good friend.

_____ I'm funny.   _____ I'm kind.

_____ I'm determined.   _____ I'm a good listener.

_____ I'm a good parent.   _____ I'm attractive.

_____ I'm always on time.   _____ I'm a good partner.

_____ I have a good voice.   _____ I'm a good cook.

_____ I'm creative.   _____ I live a healthy life.

_____ I have a good memory   _____ I'm helpful.

_____ I'm athletic.   _____ I'm strong.

What other positive traits do you have? Write them in the space provided.

Be Proud!

Look at the list above. These are some of the things that you do very well. Be proud of yourself! Not everyone could write this list. Not everyone is as good as you are at these things. Always remember that you are a valuable person!

Take a Good Look at the Negative

People with high self-esteem know that they are not perfect. They know they have some **negative**, or bad, traits. These are things that they would like to change about themselves.

In order to change your self-esteem, you need to think about your negative traits. You need to think about things you would like to improve.

What About You?

1. Listed below are some negative traits. Put a check mark next to the traits that you possess.

_____ I don't have a healthy lifestyle.

_____ I lose my temper often.

_____ I am always late.

_____ I ignore people.

_____ I don't exercise enough.

_____ I spend too much money.

_____ I give up easily.

_____ I don't let others know I care about them.

_____ I don't take care of my things.

_____ I put my needs ahead of the needs of others.

_____ I need to be in control.

_____ I don't accept others who are different from me.

_____ I gamble.

_____ I drink too much.

_____ I smoke.

_____ I'm not dependable.

2. Do you possess any negative traits not listed above? Write them in the space provided.

3. Look over the traits you checked on the previous page. Choose three traits that you would most like to change. Write these traits in the space provided.

    a.

    b.

    c.

Think About Why You Want to Change

You have already taken the first two steps toward changing your self-esteem. You have named your positive traits. You have also named some things that you would like to change about yourself.

Your next step is thinking about *why* you want to change some things about yourself. Is the change something you want to do for yourself? Or is the change something you want to do for others?

What About You?

At the top of this page, you listed three things you would most like to change about yourself. Think about why you want to make these changes. Write your reasons in the space provided.

13

Get Ready for a Change

You should feel very proud of yourself! You have just taken some important steps toward raising your self-esteem. You have thought about the things you do well. You have named things you would like to improve. You have thought about why you want to make these changes. The last thing you must do is believe that you have the power to change. The rest of this book will show you how to make the changes you want. It won't be easy. It will take some effort. Is it worth it?

Definitely. Remember, you deserve the *best*.

Check What You've Learned

Read each statement. If the statement is true, write T on the answer blank. If the statement is false, write F on the answer blank. (Check your answers on page 116.)

_____ **1.** Self-esteem cannot be changed.

_____ **2.** People with high self-esteem have only positive traits.

_____ **3.** Negative traits are things you'd like to change about yourself.

_____ **4.** You should want to change for yourself, not for others.

_____ **5.** Raising self-esteem means believing that you have the power to change.

Unit 1 Review

In this unit: _____

- You learned that self-esteem is your opinion of yourself. People with high self-esteem value themselves and their abilities. They are comfortable with themselves.

- You discovered that goals are things you hope to achieve. High self-esteem helps you reach your goals. By believing in yourself and your abilities, you are willing to try to obtain the things you want.

- You recognized that self-esteem can be changed. To change your self-esteem, you need to think about who you are. You need to name your positive traits. You need to think about what you'd like to change about yourself. You need to think about why you want to make these changes.

Key Words _____

Match each word in Column A with the correct meaning in Column B. Write the letter from Column B on the answer blank in Column A. (Check your answers on page 116.)

Column A

_____ **1.** goal

_____ **2.** negative

_____ **3.** positive

_____ **4.** self-esteem

Column B

a. good; healthy

b. your opinion of yourself

c. something you hope to achieve

d. bad; harmful

Key Ideas _____

Write the answer to each question in the space provided.
(Check your answers on page 116.)

1. What is self-esteem?

2. Explain how people with high self-esteem feel about themselves.

3. Explain how people with low self-esteem feel about themselves.

4. What are goals?

5. Does everybody have the same goals? Explain.

6. How does high self-esteem help you reach your goals?

7. How does low self-esteem stop you from reaching your goals?

8. What are three things you should do to change your self-esteem?

What About You? _____

Think about what you learned in Unit 1. What information do you plan to use in your daily life? Explain.

Strengths and Weaknesses

In this unit you will:

- discover how being positive helps self-esteem.
- identify your strengths and weaknesses.
- practice turning weaknesses into strengths.

Key Words

strengths: good qualities that you like about yourself
weaknesses: bad qualities that you do not like about yourself

More About Jack Carter

Remember Jack Carter? You read about him in Unit 1. He lost his job at a nursing home. He was fired because he spent too much time talking with the people who lived there.

Jack needed to find another job. He remembered what his boss had said. He had said that Jack "had a way with people." Jack thought a lot about those words. They made him feel good. They made him feel special.

Jack knows that he is good at working with older people. But this ability does not make him suited for the job in the laundry room. It kept him from doing his work. That was why he had been fired.

But Jack's ability is good for other kinds of jobs. His boss knew this too. That's why he told Jack that he would let him know if a job as an aide became available. An aide works with the elderly to help take care of their needs. An aide helps an elderly person get dressed, cleaned up and get from place to place. Most important, an aide listens to an elderly person. The aide becomes the person's friend. These are all things that Jack could do very well.

Think About It

Circle the letter of the statement that best completes each sentence. (Check your answers on page 116.)

1. Jack knows that he is good at
   a. doing laundry.
   b. cleaning.
   c. working with people.
   d. being a boss.

2. Jack's special ability is suited for a job as a(n)
   a. driver.
   b. waiter.
   c. cleaner.
   d. aide.

Be Positive

Jack Carter decided to look for another job. He knew that he wanted to work with the elderly. Jack wanted a job in which he could use his special ability.

Jack started his job search by reading the want ads. But none of them described the kind of job he wanted.

The next thing Jack did was make a list of places in his community that served the elderly. At the top of his list was the local senior citizen office. Next came another nursing home, a medical center, and a drugstore. Jack decided to go to each place on his list.

Jack planned to ask whether there were any jobs open. He went to the senior citizen office first. The office was on the first floor of a large building. Jack felt a little uncomfortable as he walked in. "What am I going to say?" he wondered. "'Can I have a job?' seemed a bit silly," he thought.

"Can I help you?" said a woman sitting behind the counter. Jack felt really silly. He almost turned around.

Then Jack thought about the bills that would be coming in at the end of the month. "I was wondering if you had any jobs available," he blurted.

"What kind of job are you looking for?" the woman asked.

"I'm not sure," said Jack. "All I know is that I'd like a job working with the elderly. I used to work in a nursing home. I liked that job very much."

"Why not come back here," said the woman. "My name is Mrs. Rogers. I'm the office manager. You just might be the person I'm looking for."

Jack walked back behind the counter. He sat down and told Mrs. Rogers about his old job. He explained why he had been let go. Jack told Mrs. Rogers that she could call his boss at the nursing home. He would explain what had happened.

Mrs. Rogers did call Jack's boss. He told her that Jack's story was correct. He told her that Jack had a good way with the elderly.

Mrs. Rogers smiled as she hung up the phone. "Jack, I have good news for you. I like what your boss just told me. I think I have a job that would allow you to use your special abilities. How soon could you start?"

"How about today?" Jack answered eagerly.

Think About It

How did Jack's boss help Jack get the job? (Check your answer on page 116.)

Concentrate on Your Good Points

Jack was lucky. He was able to find another job. His new job and his abilities are a good match.

How did Jack do this? Jack was positive. He knew that he was good at some things. He concentrated on his good points.

Jack looked for a job where he could use his abilities. He thought about himself in a positive way. Then he presented himself in a positive way to Mrs. Rogers. He sent her a clear message. He told her, "I have a good way with the elderly."

Mrs. Rogers heard Jack's message. She checked it with his boss. She decided that Jack's ability was something she could use in the senior citizen office.

Be Honest With Yourself and Others

Jack did something else. He was honest. He was truthful to himself. Jack does not think that he is good at everything. He knows that there are some things he doesn't do well.

Jack was also honest with Mrs. Rogers. He told her he had a way with the elderly. He did not boast. Jack told

Mrs. Rogers the truth about losing his job. He did not blame his boss. He did not say that he quit. Jack told Mrs. Rogers that he had been fired. Then he explained to Mrs. Rogers why he had lost the job.

Jack also told Mrs. Rogers to call his boss. He wanted her to be sure that he was telling the truth. Jack knew that his boss would tell her the same story. He wanted Mrs. Rogers to be sure of his ability. Jack's honesty helped him get the job.

Think About It

Suppose Jack had told Mrs. Rogers that he had quit the nursing home because he didn't get paid enough. Suppose Mrs. Rogers then called Jack's boss, who told her the truth about why Jack left the nursing home. Do you think that Mrs. Rogers would have hired Jack if this had happened? Explain. (Check your answer on page 116.)

What About You?

Rate yourself in each of the following abilities. Circle the number that best describes you.

1. My ability to work with young children is

5	4	3	2	1
Great		Average		Poor

2. My ability to work with the elderly is

5	4	3	2	1
Great		Average		Poor

3. My ability to work with animals is

5	4	3	2	1
Great		Average		Poor

4. My ability to work with sick people is

5	4	3	2	1
Great		Average		Poor

5. My ability to work in an office is

5	4	3	2	1
Great		Average		Poor

6. My ability to make things with my hands is

5 Great	4	3 Average	2	1 Poor

7. My ability to work with machines is

5 Great	4	3 Average	2	1 Poor

Look over the numbers you circled. Did you circle 4 or 5 for any statement? If so, you named some of your special abilities. Write these abilities in the space provided. Then name a job that is suited for each ability.

Ability   **Job**

Check What You've Learned

Read each statement. If the statement is true, write T on the answer blank. If the statement is false, write F on the answer blank. (Check your answers on page 116.)

_____ **1.** Being positive means thinking that you are good at everything.

_____ **2.** A positive person brags about his or her special abilities.

_____ **3.** A positive person is honest with himself or herself.

Identify Your Strengths and Weaknesses

No one is perfect. Everyone has some good points. Everyone has some bad points.

Everyone Has Strengths

Your good points are your strengths. **Strengths** are good qualities that you like about yourself. They are things that make you feel proud. Your strengths make you different from other people. Your strengths are things that make you special.

What About You?

Thinking about your strengths will help raise your self-esteem. It will help you be positive.

Read each heading in the box below. Think about how the heading applies to you. In the spaces inside the box, name your strengths.

MY STRENGTHS	
Things I Do Well	**Things I Am Interested In**
Things I Have Achieved	**What I Like About My Looks**

Everyone Has Weaknesses

Now it's time to think about your bad points. Everyone has bad points. Your bad points are called weaknesses. **Weaknesses** are bad qualities that you would like to change about yourself.

People with high self-esteem know that they have certain weaknesses. They accept their weaknesses. They don't blame themselves for having these bad points.

Does that mean never working to improve yourself? Absolutely not. You should always work to be the best you can. You should always work to improve your weaknesses.

What About You?

Read each heading in the box below. Think about how the heading applies to you. In the spaces inside the box, name your weaknesses.

MY WEAKNESSES	
Things I Cannot Do	**Things I Am Not Interested In**
Things I Am Afraid to Try	**What I Dislike About My Looks**

Concentrate on Your Strengths

In the last lesson, you named some of your strengths. Start off each day thinking about one of your strengths. Make an effort to use the strength during your daily activities. Show others that you possess this good point.

Suppose one of your strengths is that you are a good cook. You could use this strength by making dinner for a friend. Or you could volunteer to work in the kitchen of a shelter for the homeless.

Perhaps one of your strengths is that you are good at basketball. Why not use this ability by teaching a youngster how to play the game? Or you could volunteer to coach in an after-school program.

Maybe you have a way with young children. You could use this strength by baby-sitting for a friend's children. Or you could do some volunteer work in a day care center.

Learning to make the most of your strengths has many benefits. Using your strengths will help make you feel good about yourself. It will be a reminder that you are special and valuable. This will keep your self-esteem high.

You can use your strengths to help others. People around you will recognize your special abilities. They will look upon you in a favorable way. You will receive this message. It will help your self-esteem grow.

What About You?

Think about a time when you used a strength. Answer these questions about that time.

1. Which of your strengths did you show others?

2. How did you use this strength?

3. How did other people treat you?

4. How did this make you feel?

Think About It

Each of the following people has certain strengths. Think about how they could use these special abilities. Suggest ways that they could show others their strengths. (Check your answers on page 116.)

1. Marlo is good at art. She can draw very well.

2. Franklin loves to work on car engines. He is very good at fixing cars that have engine problems.

3. Scott enjoys working with young children. He does not have children of his own. Scott would like to spend time with some children in the neighborhood.

4. Debbi is a good reader. She reads the entire newspaper every day.

Turn Weaknesses Into Strengths

So far, you have been concentrating on your strengths. But what about your weaknesses? Do you just forget about them?

No. You try to turn them into strengths. That is exactly what Jack did. His friendliness with the elderly was considered a weakness in his old job. This ability was not suited to working in the laundry room. There it was thought to be a weakness.

However, being friendly to people is a strength in other situations. Jack knew that. He looked for a job where this ability would be helpful. He turned a weakness into a strength.

Maybe one of your weaknesses is that you are always cleaning up around your home. You just cannot sit still until everything is in its place. You need things to be neat and orderly.

This weakness might be hard for others to live with. But it would definitely help a cleaning person do his or her job. In that job, being very neat and orderly would be a strength.

Think About It

Read about each person. Think of how their weaknesses could be turned into strengths. Describe your thoughts in the space provided. (Check your answers on page 116.)

1. Martha loves to talk. She spends much of her day talking on the telephone.

2. Zack is always taking things apart. He likes to see just how things work.

3. Marcelle's husband tells her that she is too organized. He thinks that Marcelle spends too much time making sure that everything is in its proper place.

Accept the Things You Cannot Change

Not every weakness can be made into a strength. Some things cannot be changed. Learn to accept these things about yourself. Say to yourself, "I know that I have some weaknesses. But even with these weaknesses, I am still a valuable person. There are many more good things about me than bad." Then believe it.

Unit 2 Review

In this unit:

- You discovered that being positive helps boost self-esteem. Being positive means knowing that you have good points. Being positive means showing others that you have certain abilities.

- You thought about your strengths or the things you like about yourself. You also thought about your weaknesses or the things you would like to change about yourself.

- You learned that using your strengths can help keep your self-esteem high. Changing your weaknesses into strengths is another way of being positive.

Key Words

Use your own words to explain the meaning of each word below. (Check your answers on page 117.)

1. strengths

2. weaknesses

Key Ideas

Write the answer to each question in the space provided. (Check your answers on page 117.)

1. Describe a person who is positive.

2. Explain the difference between a strength and a weakness.

3. Do people with high self-esteem make believe that they don't have any weaknesses? Explain your answer.

4. What does "use your strengths" mean?

5. Can all weaknesses be turned into strengths? Explain.

What About You? _____

Name two of the most important things you learned in Unit 2. Explain how you will use this information in your everyday life.

Real-World Connection

The Neat Freak

Carla put the last dish into the **cabinet**. She glanced at her watch. "I'd better get a move on!" she thought. Tito would be picking her up in five minutes. She wasn't even dressed yet!

Just then, the doorbell rang. "Great," Carla thought. "Tito's early!"

She opened the door. One look told Tito that she wasn't ready to leave. He was **furious**!

"I've had it, Carla," he said. "I'm tired of waiting for you! You're always late!"

"It's not my fault," Carla answered. "I had to clean up the kitchen. I just finished a minute ago."

"That's the problem," Tito yelled. "You just can't let anything go. You have to make sure that everything's **perfect**! You're a neat freak!"

These words hurt Carla. She was angry. "I am *not* a neat freak!" she **replied**. "I just like to keep everything clean. Is that such a crime?"

"It is when it makes you late all the time," Tito said. "Now we'll never get to the store before it closes!"

"Yes, we will," she said. "Just give me two minutes." Then she ran into her bedroom.

Carla **reappeared** quickly. "Let's go," she said.

They made it to the store before it closed. As they walked through the door, Carla **noticed** a sign. It said, "Help Wanted."

Tito noticed the sign also. "Why not ask about the job," he said. "You've been looking for work."

Carla asked the manager about the job. He told her that he needed a file clerk. That person would have to keep all the store's files **organized** and neat.

"I'd like to **apply** for the job," Carla said. "I think I would be very good at it."

"What makes you say that?" asked the manager.

"I like to keep things in good order," said Carla. "It's something I've always done. Sometimes, my need for order gets in the way of my schedule."

Tito spoke up. "Let me tell you something," he said. "She is really **suited** for this job. She's a total neat freak!"

The manager thought about it. He asked Carla a few more questions. Then he asked when she could start work.

"Next week," she replied.

"Great. You have the job. Your first day is Monday. The store opens at ten."

On their way out of the store, Carla turned to Tito. "I guess being a neat freak isn't bad all the time."

"You're right," Tito said. "That **trait** of yours just got you a job."

Key Words

In the story, 10 words are in **bold print**. These words are listed below. Circle the letter of the correct meaning for each word. If you have trouble, go back and read the sentence containing the word. Look for clues in the sentence. Use the clues to figure out the meaning of the words.
(Check your answers on page 117.)

1. **Cabinet** means
   a. building.
   b. sink.
   c. cupboard.
   d. window.

2. **Furious** means
   a. angry.
   b. happy.
   c. worried.
   d. sick.

3. **Perfect** means
   a. dirty.
   b. without mistakes.
   c. busy.
   d. empty.

4. **Replied** means
   a. yelled.
   b. cried.
   c. whispered.
   d. answered.

5. **Reappear** means
   a. to hide again.
   b. to walk away.
   c. to come again.
   d. to leave.

6. **Noticed** means
   a. ignored.
   b. saw.
   c. wrote.
   d. made.

7. **Organized** means
   a. arranged
   b. dusted
   c. torn
   d. scattered.

8. **Apply** means
   a. work.
   b. quit.
   c. request.
   d. miss.

9. **Suited** means
   a. terrible.
   b. clothing.
   c. wanted.
   d. good for.

10. **Trait** means
    a. quality.
    b. family.
    c. fish.
    d. measure.

Check What You've Learned _____

Circle the letter of the best answer to each question.
(Check your answers on page 117.)

1. How did Carla feel when she
   looked at her watch?
   a. Proud
   b. Happy
   c. Nervous
   d. Sick

2. Carla and Tito were going to
   a. a park.
   b. a store.
   c. a restaurant.
   d. the movies.

3. Why was Tito angry with Carla?
   a. She wasn't ready.
   b. She wants new dishes.
   c. She can't tell time.
   d. She doesn't drive.

4. Tito thinks Carla wants
   a. a dirty apartment.
   b. to get married.
   c. everything perfect.
   d. to see someone else.

5. What kind of job did Carla apply
   for?
   a. Salesperson
   b. Cleaning crew member
   c. File clerk
   d. Chair maker

6. What did Tito tell the store
   manager?
   a. Carla is always on time.
   b. Carla is suited for the job.
   c. Carla is dependable.
   d. Carla is a bad worker.

7. Both Tito and Carla
   a. noticed the Help Wanted sign.
   b. needed a new job.
   c. cleaned the apartment.
   d. applied for a job.

Think About It _____

In Unit 2 you learned how to turn a weakness into a
strength. Explain how Carla did this. (Check your answer on
page 117.)

Values

In this unit you will:

- think about your moral code.
- become aware of your values.
- understand the relationship between goals and values.

Key Words

moral code: a set of rules having to do with right and wrong
religion: a system of beliefs or worship
values: things that are important to you

Meet Jana Sokolovsky and Linda Javier

Jana Sokolovsky and Linda Javier are best friends. The two women have known each other since grade school. They feel as close as sisters.

Both women are single mothers. Neither one is working. Money is tight for the women. They usually don't have enough money to pay their bills. But somehow they manage. They do things that don't cost any money. They take walks around the neighborhood. They go to the library.

One day, the women decided to take the children to the park. The park was very crowded. It seemed as if everyone in the neighborhood had the same idea.

After a while, Jana needed to go to the rest room. She left her daughter playing in the sandbox with Linda's son. Linda said that she would watch them.

When Jana entered the rest room, she saw her neighbor Mrs. Fields. Mrs. Fields was washing her hands. The two women spoke for few minutes. Then they went their separate ways.

Soon after, Jana washed her hands. She noticed something on the floor in front of the sink Mrs. Fields had been using. It was a twenty-dollar bill. Jana scooped it up quickly and stuffed it into her pocket.

Think About It

Circle the letter of the statement that best answers the question. (Check your answer on page 117.)

1. Who is Mrs. Fields?

    a. Jana's mother

    b. the baby-sitter

    c. Linda's sister

    d. a neighbor

Right and Wrong

Jana Sokolovsky rushed back to Linda Javier. "You'll never believe what I just found!" she squealed.

"What?" asked Linda.

Jana held up the twenty-dollar bill. "This!" she exclaimed.

Linda was surprised. She was also puzzled. "How did you find it?" she asked her friend.

Jana told Linda about going into the rest room. She told her about talking with Mrs. Fields. She explained that she saw the money when she washed her hands.

Linda listened carefully to the story. A worried look came over her face.

Jana noticed it. "What's wrong?" she asked.

"Jana, I don't think you should keep that money," said Linda.

"Why not?" asked Jana.

"It isn't yours," continued Linda. "It probably is Mrs. Fields'. You said that she had been standing by the sink where you found it. She probably dropped the money while she was washing her hands."

"Great! I finally get a break and you want me to give it up!" Jana said angrily. "I don't know if it is Mrs. Fields'. I didn't see her drop it. So I'm going to keep it."

"Why not ask Mrs. Fields if she is missing some money?" suggested Linda. "That way you can find out if it is her money or not."

"Get real, Linda. Who would answer no to that question? Anyone would say yes in order to get the money," said Jana.

"Not me," replied Linda. "I would be honest. I wouldn't try to get money that wasn't mine. I just don't think that's the right thing to do."

"Well, I think differently," Jana said. "I found this money. I'm going to keep it. I'm not going to start asking around to see if anyone lost any money!"

Think About It

Circle the letter of the statement that best completes each sentence. (Check your answers on page 117.)

1. Linda thinks that Jana should
   a. put the money back.
   b. give Mrs. Fields the money.
   c. ask Mrs. Fields if she lost any money.
   d. keep the money.
2. Jana decided to
   a. talk to Mrs. Fields.
   b. keep the money.
   c. talk to a police officer.
   d. split the money with Linda.

Moral Codes

In the last unit, you learned that people with high self-esteem know their strengths and weaknesses. They accept that they are not perfect at everything they do.

People with high self-esteem know themselves quite well. They know who they are. They know what they want to be. They understand themselves.

The first step in figuring out who you are is to decide what is right and what is wrong. A set of rules for right and wrong is sometimes called a **moral code**.

A moral code is a personal thing. It is made up by you. It is based on your family's and your culture's beliefs. Different people have different moral codes.

Jana and Linda are very good friends. They are alike in many ways. But they have different moral codes. Jana thinks that it is okay to keep the money she found. Linda thinks that it is not right. She thinks that Jana should ask Mrs. Fields whether the money is hers. The women think differently because their moral codes are different.

What do you think Jana should do with the money? Explain.

What Affects Your Moral Code?

Different people have different moral codes. That's because people are different. They come from different families. They had different childhoods. They have different friends. They have different life experiences.

All of these factors affect your moral code. They determine what you think is wrong and right.

Something else affects your moral code: your religion. **Religion** is a system of beliefs. It is a system of worship. There are many different religions. Each religion has its own set of beliefs about what is right and what is wrong.

In order to know yourself, you need to think about your moral code. You need to think about your own rules for what is right and wrong. You also need to think about the reasons you feel this way.

What About You?

Listed below are some things that might affect your moral code. Put a *1* next to the item that has the greatest effect on your code. Put a *2* next to the item that has the next-greatest effect on you. Continue in this manner until you have put a number next to each statement. A *5* should appear next to the item that has the least effect on your moral code.

_____ My religion

_____ My family

_____ My friends

_____ My partner

_____ Laws

Does anything else affect your moral code? List these factors in the space provided.

Think About It

Spend a few moments thinking about your moral code by completing each sentence. Write your answers in the space provided.

1. As a friend, I think it is right to

2. As a friend, I think it is wrong to

3. As a partner, I think it is right to

4. As a partner, I think it is wrong to

5. As a neighbor, I think it is right to

6. As a neighbor, I think it is wrong to

7. As a citizen, I think it is right to

8. As a citizen, I think it is wrong to

Check What You've Learned

Read each statement. If the statement is true, write T on the answer blank. If the statement is false, write F on the answer blank. (Check your answers on page 117.)

_____ 1. A moral code is a personal thing.

_____ 2. Your family and friends affect your moral code.

_____ 3. Religion is a system of beliefs or worship.

_____ 4. Religion does not affect your moral code.

Know Your Values

In order to get to know yourself, you need to think about your values. **Values** are things that are important to you. Many of the choices you make are based upon your values.

Think back to Jana Sokolovsky and Linda Javier. They had a difference of opinion about what Jana should do with the money she found. The women also had different values. Having money was extremely important to Jana. It was also important to Linda. However, equally important to Linda was being kind to people. She felt strongly that you should treat people the way you want them to treat you.

Linda thought about how she would feel if she were Mrs. Fields. She would want Jana to ask her whether she had lost the money. Linda would be honest in her response. She wouldn't claim the money unless she had really lost it.

What About You?

Listed below are some common values. Put a check mark on the answer blank next to the values that are important to you.

_____ Having money   _____ Having a family

_____ Wearing nice clothes   _____ Being nice to others

_____ Having a lot of friends   _____ Spending time alone

_____ Being in love   _____ Being successful

_____ Taking risks   _____ Owning a car

_____ Being a good parent   _____ Being a good citizen

Would you add anything to this list? Write other values in the space provided.

Values and Decisions

Knowing your values can help you make decisions. All through your life, you are faced with choices. Some choices are easy. Deciding what to eat for dinner is easy. Other choices are hard. For example, deciding about ending a relationship is hard.

Thinking about your values helps you make hard decisions. By knowing your values, you can make choices that you can live with. You can make decisions that you won't regret later.

Whenever you face a hard decision, think about your values. Say to yourself, "What is important to me? Which choice will help me get the things I feel I need?" Then make your decision.

Think About It

Read about each person below. Decide what you would do in the same situation. In the space provided, describe why you made your decision.

1. Darla promised her sister that she would watch her baby on Saturday. Darla just got a call from a man she likes very much. He asked Darla to go out Saturday night. Darla has to make a hard decision. What would you do?

2. Mike's son is in the school play. Mike has promised his son that he will go see the play tonight. Mike's boss has asked Mike to work overtime. If Mike stays late at work, he will miss the play. Since tonight is the last performance, Mike has to make a hard decision. What would you do?

3. Joan has $35 to pay the telephone bill. If she doesn't pay this month, the company will turn off her phone. On her way to pay the bill, Joan notices that her favorite shoe store is having a sale. A pair of boots that Joan really wants is on sale at half price. Joan has enough money for the boots. But if she buys them, she will not be able to pay the telephone bill. Joan has a hard decision to make. What would you do?

Check What You've Learned

Read each statement. If the statement is true, write T on the answer blank. If the statement is false, write F on the answer blank. (Check your answers on page 117.)

_____ **1.** People all have the same values.

_____ **2.** Values affect the choices you make.

_____ **3.** Knowing your values helps you make wise decisions.

Goals and Values

In the last lesson, you learned that values are things that are important to you. Your values lead to your goals. Goals are things you want to achieve. Goals are the things you work toward.

Values and goals are connected. The things you are working toward, or goals, should be things that you think are important. They should reflect your values. Having a clear understanding of yourself will help to keep your goals and values linked.

What About You?

Look back at the values you checked on page 40. Choose two of these values. Write the values in the space provided.

Value 1:

Value 2:

Now think about a goal that would fit with each value listed above. For example, suppose one of your values is to be healthy. A goal that would help you express this value is to take a walk every evening. Think about your two values. Write a goal for each value in the space provided.

Goal for Value 1:

Goal for Value 2:

Goals and Self-Esteem

Your self-esteem can help you to reach your goals. Or it can keep you from achieving what you want. It all depends on whether your self-esteem is high or low.

People with high self-esteem are willing to try new things. They believe in themselves. They feel powerful. They take chances because they believe that they are going to be successful.

People with high self-esteem do not always reach their goals. Sometimes they make mistakes. Sometimes they fail. But they don't give up. They learn from their mistakes. They try again. Eventually, with a little effort, they reach their goals.

People with low self-esteem often do not meet their goals. Why? They don't believe in themselves. They are afraid to try new things. They think "Why bother? I won't be able to do it well. I never do anything well. It's not worth the effort." These thoughts are negative. They hold you down. Low self-esteem keeps you from becoming the person you want to be.

What About You?

Think about the last time you achieved a goal. Answer these questions about that experience.

1. What was your goal?

2. What value of yours did this goal match?

3. Did your self-esteem help you reach your goal? Explain how.

4. How did reaching your goal make you feel?

Set Reasonable Goals

When setting a personal goal, be sure that it is possible to reach. Everyone would like to be a millionaire. But it is not possible for every person to achieve that goal.

Goals should be reasonable. They should be achievable. A goal should take some effort. It should not be too easy. Goals should make you stretch a little. Instead of having a goal of being a millionaire, you might work toward the goal of paying off all your bills. This goal is possible.

Making your goals reasonable will help to build your self-esteem. You will work toward something you want. You will achieve it. This will give you a good feeling about yourself. It will make you feel proud. Your self-esteem will rise.

Check What You've Learned _____

Read each statement. If the statement is true, write T on the answer blank. If the statement is false, write F on the answer blank. (Check your answers on page 117.)

_____ 1. Goals are things you hope to achieve.

_____ 2. There is no connection between values and goals.

_____ 3. All people have the same goals.

_____ 4. Goals should be things that you can achieve easily.

_____ 5. Setting reasonable goals helps build your self-esteem.

Unit 3 Review

In this unit:

- You learned that a moral code is a set of rules having to do with right and wrong. Every person has his or her own moral code. Family, childhood, friends, religion, and laws all contribute to your moral code.

- You discovered that values are things that are important to you. Different people have different values.

- You learned that goals are things that you want to achieve. Your goals should match your values. Making reasonable goals will help keep your self-esteem high.

Key Words

Match each word in Column A with the correct meaning in Column B. Write the letter from Column B on the answer blank next to the number in Column A. (Check your answers on page 117.)

Column A	Column B
_____ **1.** moral code	**a.** things that are important to you
_____ **2.** religion	**b.** a set of rules having to do with right and wrong
_____ **3.** values	**c.** a system of beliefs or worship

Key Ideas

Write the answer to each question in the space provided. (Check your answers on page 117.)

1. Do all people have the same moral code? Explain.

2. Name four things that affect your moral code.

3. How can thinking about your values help you make wise decisions?

4. Are goals and values connected? Explain how.

5. How can high self-esteem help you reach your goals?

6. How can low self-esteem keep you from reaching your goals?

7. Describe two traits of a reasonable goal.

8. How can making reasonable goals help raise your self-esteem?

What About You? _____

What was the most important thing you learned in Unit 3? Explain how you can use this information in your everyday life.

Real-World Connection

The Letter

Paul and Kit just moved in together. Things have been going well for the **couple**. They like sharing an apartment. It gives them more time together. It makes them feel **connected**.

One day when Kit was working, the doorbell rang. Paul opened the door to find the letter carrier.

"I have a special delivery letter," she said. "Someone has to sign for it."

Paul looked at the letter. It was addressed to Kit. "OK," he said. "I'll sign for it." He **scribbled** his name on the form.

As he closed the door, Paul looked again at the envelope. He didn't **recognize** the return address.

Paul went to the telephone. He looked up Kit's work number and dialed it. Another **employee** answered. Paul waited until Kit came to the phone.

"Hello," said Kit.

"Kit, it's Paul. I wanted to let you know that you just got a special delivery letter. It might be important. Do you want me to open it?" asked Paul.

Kit was quiet. After a few seconds, Kit said, "Are you kidding me? You called me at work to tell me that?"

Paul was **confused**. Kit sounded annoyed. Paul didn't know what he had done wrong.

Before he could ask, Kit said "Just leave it on the table. I'll see it when I get home." Then the phone went dead.

A few hours later, Kit **arrived** home. Kit *was* annoyed.

Paul waited a while. Then he finally went to Kit. He asked what was wrong.

"I don't believe you called me at work," Kit said. "I've never done that to you!"

"What did I do?" asked Paul.

"You've **embarrassed** me," Kit said.

"I really don't understand the problem," said Paul. "I thought you should know about the letter. It seemed important. I figured the best thing to do was call you at work."

"Don't you know anything?" Kit replied. "It's wrong to call a person at work unless it's an emergency."

"It is not!" Paul said angrily. "When I was a kid, I called my father at work every day. As soon as I got home, I'd dial his number. He *wanted* me to call. That way he knew where I was!"

"Well, in my house we were **forbidden** to call our parents at work. We were told it could get them in trouble," responded Kit.

The roommates looked at each other. They thought about what each one had just said. Paul smiled.

"I guess we just figured out the problem," he said. "Your family thought calling someone at work was wrong. My family thought it was normal."

Kit smiled. "We grew up in different places. We lived with different families. I guess that we have different feelings on some things. That's OK, we'll just have to learn to respect our differences!"

Key Words

In the story, nine words are in **bold print**. These words are listed below. Circle the letter of the correct meaning for each word. If you have trouble, go back and read the sentence containing the word. Look for clues in the sentence. Use the clues to figure out the meaning of the word. (Check your answers on page 117.)

1. **Couple** means
   a. man.
   b. group of people.
   c. two people.
   d. person.

2. **Connected** means
   a. alone.
   b. joined.
   c. happy.
   d. separate.

3. **Scribble** means
   a. to yell.
   b. to move slowly.
   c. to write quickly.
   d. to cry.

4. **Recognize** means
   a. to see.
   b. to question.
   c. to destroy
   d. to know.

5. **Employee** means
   a. boss.
   b. customer.
   c. worker.
   d. manager.

6. **Confused** means
   a. brave.
   b. mixed up.
   c. well liked.
   d. set straight.

7. **Arrive** means
   a. to reach a place.
   b. to leave.
   c. to walk.
   d. to bend.

8. **Embarrassed** means
   a. smiled.
   b. laughed.
   c. ashamed.
   d. helped.

9. **Forbidden** means
   a. allowed.
   b. encouraged.
   c. not permitted.
   d. wanted.

Check What You've Learned

Circle the letter of the best answer to each question.
(Check your answers on page 117.)

1. Kit and Paul are
   a. parents
   b. cousins.
   c. roommates.
   d. neighbors.

2. Who was at the door?
   a. Paul's father
   b. the letter carrier
   c. Kit's boss
   d. Kit's sister

3. What did Paul do when he got the letter?
   a. Opened it
   b. Read it
   c. Called his father
   d. Called Kit

4. What word describes how Kit's words made Paul feel?
   a. Confused
   b. Smart
   c. Comfortable
   d. Happy

5. According to Kit, it is
   a. normal to call a person at work.
   b. wrong to call a person at work.
   c. exciting to receive a call at work.
   d. silly to open someone else's mail.

6. As a child, Paul
   a. called his father every day.
   b. visited his father's office often.
   c. was forbidden to use the telephone.
   d. called Kit often.

7. Why did Paul smile?
   a. He was happy.
   b. He was confused.
   c. He understood the problem.
   d. He wanted a new roommate.

Think About It

In Unit 3 you learned why people have different values. Explain how Paul's and Kit's values caused their disagreement. (Check your answer on page 117.)

UNIT 4

Goals

In this unit you will:

- practice making reasonable goals.
- identify your personal goals.
- find out how to set up a plan for reaching your goals.

Key Words

plan: a series of steps for accomplishing a goal
schedule: a time line for getting something done

Meet Tia Baumann

In two months, Tia Baumann was going to be in her friend's wedding. Tia was very excited. It would be the first time she had taken part in a wedding.

Tia wanted to look good for the wedding. One day she stood in front of the mirror. She looked carefully at her reflection. Tia thought about what she could do to improve her appearance.

She decided that she needed to lose 10 pounds. Tia thought about how she could lose the weight. She decided to go on a crash diet. She would eat only one meal a day for the next two weeks.

Tia began the diet immediately. All she ate the first day was a cheeseburger at dinner time. The rest of the day, she drank only diet soda.

That night, Tia went to bed hungry. She woke up hungry. But she did not eat any breakfast. She did drink some diet soda.

By the afternoon, Tia began to feel sluggish. She was very tired. She also was very hungry.

At dinner, Tia had some meat and a few vegetables. That was all. Except, of course, for the diet soda.

The next morning Tia looked at herself in the mirror. She didn't notice any change in the shape of her body. "Why haven't I lost any weight?" she thought to herself. "I've hardly eaten anything for two days! The weight should be coming off by now!"

Her appearance made Tia angry. The fact that she was starving also made her mad. But Tia kept to the diet. She skipped breakfast. She skipped lunch. She had only a sandwich for dinner.

Think About It

Circle the letter of the statement that best completes each sentence. (Check your answers on page 117.)

1. Tia seems to value
   a. eating good food.
   b. being a good friend.
   c. looking good.
   d. being healthy.

2. Tia's goal is to
   a. get married.
   b. learn how to cook.
   c. dress better.
   d. lose 10 pounds.

Set Goals

On the fourth morning of her diet, Tia woke up with a terrible headache. She felt horrible. Her head was pounding. Her body felt weak. She was starving!

Once again, Tia stood in front of her mirror. She searched for signs of weight loss. But she did not notice any! If anything, Tia thought she looked worse than the day she started the diet.

Tia was furious. She gave up! She went into the kitchen. She ate everything she could get her hands on. Cookies, chips, even ice cream for breakfast!

Then Tia called her friend, the woman who was getting married. She told her friend that something had come up. She would not be able to be in the wedding. When her friend asked why, Tia said, "I'll just embarrass you."

Her friend tried to change Tia's mind. She told Tia that she really wanted Tia to be a part of her special day. But Tia's mind was made up. There was no way that she would be part of the wedding.

Tia hung up the telephone. She went back to bed. She just lay there, staring at the ceiling. Tia felt like a big failure. "It was stupid of me to think that I would be able to stick to a diet," she thought. "I never do anything right. Why would I be able to lose weight?"

Then Tia cried herself to sleep.

Think About It

Circle the letter of the statement that best completes each sentence. (Check your answers on page 117.)

1. Tia decided not to be in her friend's wedding because

    a. she had nothing to wear.

    b. she thought she was unattractive.

    c. her friend was mean to her.

    d. she had an argument with her friend.

2. Stopping the diet made Tia feel

    a. like a failure.

    b. good about herself.

    c. powerful.

    d. happy to be in the wedding.

3. Do you think Tia has high or low self-esteem? Explain.

Set Reasonable Goals

In Unit 3 you learned about how to set good goals. A good goal is something that fits in with your values. It is also something that makes you stretch a little. A good goal is also reasonable.

A reasonable goal is something that you have a chance of doing. It is possible. A reasonable goal is not easy. It takes some time. It takes some work. But it can be done.

Think about Tia's goal to lose weight. She decided to lose 10 pounds. This goal fit in with her values. Tia values looking good for her friend's wedding. Losing weight connects with this value.

Trying to lose weight is something that makes you stretch a bit. It is not automatic. It is not easy. It takes energy. It is work.

Tia's goal was a good goal in two ways. First, it fit with her values. Second, it made her stretch.

But Tia did not approach the goal in a reasonable way. She wanted to lose the weight in a few days. She decided to starve herself in order to shed some pounds. This is not possible!

Because she did not approach the goal in an achievable manner, Tia failed.

Make a Plan

How could Tia have reached her goal? She should have made a plan. A **plan** is a series of steps. Each step is one small action. Each step leads to the next step. By taking each step one at a time, you reach your goal.

Tia should have broken down her goal of losing weight into small steps. One step would be to eat wisely. That means eating three meals a day. Not one! It also means eating the right kind of food. Tia should have thought about what she would eat for each meal. She should have included different kinds of foods, such as fruits and vegetables, in her meals. She should have cut out fats and sugars. Tia definitely should have cut back on the amount of junk food she ate and the diet soda she drank.

Tia also should have included exercise in her plan for losing weight. Exercise helps burn off extra calories. It helps keep your body fit and healthy.

Think About It

What other advice would you give Tia about the right way to lose weight?

Allow Enough Time

Tia could have started walking every day. She could have walked for 15 minutes each day. Then she could have increased the amount of time to 20 minutes or a half hour. She could have cut out some fats and sweets. In fact, she could have cut out all sweets. Most important, Tia needed to do these things gradually!

That was Tia's other mistake. She did not give herself enough time to lose weight. She wanted to accomplish her goal quickly. Tia should have given herself some time to reach her goal. It would have been more reasonable. It would have increased the likelihood that Tia would accomplish her goal.

Keep to a Schedule

Breaking your goal down into small steps helps you reach your goal. Another important thing to do is make a schedule. A **schedule** is a time line for getting something done. With a schedule, you state when you want to finish each step. A schedule helps you use your time and your energy wisely. By making a schedule, you give yourself some idea of how long it will take to reach your goal. This helps keep you focused. It helps you accomplish your goal!

Think About It

Each person described below has a goal. Each person has made a plan for reaching that goal. Read about the plan. Decide whether or not it is a good plan. Give reasons for your decisions. (Check your answers on page 118.)

1. Matt wants to paint his room. He decides to stay up all night until he finishes the job.

   Is this a good plan?

   Reasons

2. Ricky decides to start jogging. He plans to jog five miles every day for the first five days. Then he plans to increase the distance to eight miles.

   Is this a good plan?

   Reasons

3. Tara wants to clean out her closet. She decides to make a plan. Every day, she will spend 30 minutes working on the closet. First, she will organize her shoes. Next, she will go through her clothes and get rid of anything that she doesn't wear. Finally, she will arrange what is left.

Is this a good plan?

Reasons

4. Jon wants to be a better reader. He decides to read for 30 minutes each day. Jon goes to the local library. He asks the librarian to give him some books that are hard to read. These are the books Jon will read each night.

Is this a good plan?

Reasons

5. Doug wants to start playing basketball again. He used to play basketball when he was a kid. He even made his school team. But that was a long time ago. Doug decides to join a neighborhood basketball league. The team's first game is tonight. Doug is a little nervous. He hasn't touched a basketball in years!

Is this a good plan?

Reasons

6. Maria has a good singing voice. She would like to use her special ability more. She decides to try out for her church choir. Her tryout is scheduled for next week. Every day between now and then, Maria plans to spend 20 minutes singing her audition song.

Is this a good plan?

Reasons

7. Go back to the list and select one person who did not have a good plan. Think about how that plan should be changed. In the space provided, write a letter to the person and give him or her some suggestions for making a better plan.

Dear _____,

Check What You've Learned

Circle the letter of the statement that shows a reasonable schedule. (Check your answers on page 118.)

1. a. I will wash every window in my home today. I won't stop until every window is done.

   b. I will wash two windows each day. By the end of the week, all the windows will be clean.

2. a. I want to try to knit a sweater. I'll begin by buying a book and some cheap yarn. I'll practice on this until I'm sure I know what I'm doing. Then I'll buy more expensive yarn and a pattern to make the sweater I'd like.

   b. I will try to knit a sweater. I'll buy a book and all the yarn I need. Then I'll just keep working on it.

3. a. I want to eat better-balanced meals. First, I'll concentrate on breakfast. I'll try to eat good food for breakfast for three days. Then, I'll work on lunch for three days. Finally, I'll work on dinner.

   b. I want to eat better-balanced meals. Starting tomorrow, I'll cook different kinds of food for each meal. In just two days, I'll be eating healthy!

Read each statement. If the statement is true, write T on the answer blank. If the statement is false, write F on the answer blank.

_____ **4.** You should always try to reach your goals quickly.

_____ **5.** It helps to break down your goals into a series of smaller steps.

_____ **6.** The steps in a plan are all connected.

_____ **7.** When you make a schedule, you state when you want to accomplish each step of your plan.

_____ **8.** Making a schedule helps keep you focused on your plan.

LESSON 11

Set Goals: Your Turn

You have just learned about the traits of a good goal. You have also learned that making a plan helps you accomplish your goal. You found that a schedule helps to keep you focused on your goal.

Now it is time to put to use what you have learned. In this lesson, you will work on setting reasonable goals for yourself. You will also plan how you will accomplish each goal. Last, you will make a schedule for finishing each part of your plan.

Step 1: Think About Your Values

Think about your values. Name the two things that are *most* important to you.

Value 1:

Value 2:

Step 2: Write Your Goals

Now you need goals that fit with each value above. Be sure that your goals are things that you will have to work for. Be sure that they are reasonable!

Goal 1:

Goal 2:

Step 3: Make a Plan and Schedule

Next you need to make a plan for achieving your goals. Break down each goal into about five small steps. Next to each step, write the date by which it should be done.

PLAN FOR GOAL 1

Step	When It Will Be Finished
1.	
2.	
3.	
4.	
5.	

PLAN FOR GOAL 2

Step	When It Will Be Finished
1.	
2.	
3.	
4.	
5.	

Unit 4 Review

In this unit:

- You learned about making reasonable goals. You found that a reasonable goal matches your values. Reasonable goals make you stretch a bit. Reasonable goals also are achievable.

- You discovered that breaking down a goal into small steps helps to accomplish the goal. Making a plan and keeping to a schedule also help you achieve your goals.

- You identified two of your most important values. You wrote goals that matched your values. You made a plan for accomplishing each goal.

Key Words

Use your own words to explain the meaning of the following terms. (Check your answers on page 118.)

1. plan

2. schedule

Key Ideas _____

Write the answer to each question in the space provided. (Check your answers on page 118.)

1. What are three traits of a reasonable goal?

2. How does making a plan help you reach your goals?

3. How does a schedule help you reach your goals?

What About You? _____

Think about the last time you failed to reach a goal you set for yourself. Answer these questions about that experience.

1. What was your goal?

2. Did this goal match a value of yours? Explain.

3. Did the goal have all the traits of a good goal? Explain.

4. Suppose you wanted to try to reach the goal again. Make a plan for reaching that goal.

   Steps   **Time line**

Belonging

In this unit you will:

- discover the relationship between belonging and self-esteem.
- learn the steps to finding positive ways to belong.
- understand how peer pressure can cause you to make bad choices.

Key Words

community: any group that lives in the same place or has common interests

peer pressure: power used by friends to get you to do something or to act in a certain way

Meet Carol Domenici and Jude Holmes

Carol Domenici sat on her bed and sighed. She felt so tired! She didn't seem to have the energy to do anything. It was only 7 P.M., and all Carol wanted to do was sleep.

Carol's roommate, Jude Holmes, knocked on her door. "Carol, I'm going out tonight. Do you want to come along?"

Without even thinking about the offer, Carol said, "No." She turned over in bed and pulled the covers up.

Suddenly, the light flipped on. Jude was standing near the bed. "Carol," she said. "Look at you! It's only seven o'clock and you're in bed. What's going on here?"

"Nothing," Carol replied. "I'm just tired."

Jude sat down. "Look, Carol," she said. "I have to talk to you about something. I'm very worried about you. Ever since Mike broke up with you, you haven't been yourself. It seems as if you don't like to do anything anymore. All you ever do is go to work, eat dinner, and go to bed."

"If that's what makes me happy, then I should be able to do it," Carol replied angrily.

"That's the point," said Jude. "I really don't think this way of living is making you happy. You seem to be constantly bored. You hardly ever smile. I can't remember when I heard you laugh." Then she asked her friend, "Are you really happy?"

Think About It _____

Circle the letter of the best answer to the question. (Check your answer on page 118.)

Why is Jude worried about Carol?

    a. Carol is sick.

    b. Carol doesn't have a boyfriend.

    c. Carol doesn't like going out.

    d. Carol doesn't seem to be happy.

LESSON 12

The Importance of Belonging

Carol Domenici sat up. She thought about whether she was happy. Then she started to cry.

"No, I'm miserable," she said to Jude. "Life doesn't seem to be very interesting anymore. Since Mike broke up with me, I just don't know what to do with myself."

"That's normal," Jude told her. "You and Mike had been together for a long time. You probably forgot what it's like to think just for yourself. But that's what you need to do. You need to think about what *you* like to do. You need to think about what kind of life you want for yourself. Then you have to find the energy to work for it."

"Sure, that's easy for you to say," Carol said. "You've never had a guy break up with you!"

"That's not true!" Jude exclaimed. "Before we became roommates, I was seeing a guy for a long time. I really thought he was *it*! But he didn't feel the same way about me. One night, he suddenly told me that he didn't want to see me anymore. I was shocked! I didn't know how I would get on without him." Jude thought for a moment. Then she said, "But somehow I did. I made myself get out of bed and try new things. I joined a few new groups. That's how I met Al."

Carol thought about what Jude had told her. "Well," she said. "I guess I could try to do the same. But not tonight. I'll get a good rest tonight. Tomorrow, I'll think about what I'd like to do with my life."

Think About It

Circle the letter of the statement that best completes each sentence. (Check your answers on page 118.)

1. Jude knows how Carol is feeling because
   a. she read a story about someone like Carol.
   b. the same thing once happened to Jude.
   c. Jude also finds life boring.
   d. Jude once dated Mike.

2. Jude told Carol to
   a. think about the kind of life she wants for herself.
   b. stop joining new groups.
   c. be careful of men.
   d. see a doctor.

Feeling Connected

Every person needs to feel connected to others. That's because human beings are social creatures. People like to be around other people. People need to feel a link with others.

Right now, Carol does not feel connected. Why? Mike broke up with her. That made Carol feel bad. She feels unwanted. She feels worthless. Her self-esteem is low.

Luckily, Jude has given her some good advice. Carol does need to think for herself. She must think about the kind of life she wants to live. She has to find the energy to go out and make that life for herself.

What About You?

Think about a time when you felt unwanted and unvalued. Answer these questions about that time.

1. Why did you feel this way?

69

2. How did your feelings affect the way you lived your life?

3. What did you do about these feelings?

Communities

Jude also told Carol to join new groups. Why? A group will make Carol feel as if she fits in someplace. Joining a group will make Carol feel that she belongs!

Another name for a group is a community. A **community** is a group of people who have common interests. The people who live in a neighborhood make up a community. Their common interest is that they all live in the same place. A family is another kind of community. The common interest for a family is that all the members are related.

You have belonged to communities since you were born. When you were a baby, your family was your

community. When you grew older, you went to school. You became part of the school community. When you were a teen, you might have belonged to a certain group of friends. This was another kind of community.

As you age, you become a member of different kinds of communities. However, one thing is always the same. You always feel a need to belong to a community!

What About You?

1. Listed below are different kinds of communities. Put a circle around the ones that you have belonged to in the past. Put a box around the ones that you belong to now.

Family	Religious Group
Sports Team	School Community
Social Club	Neighborhood
Parent Group	Tenant Group
Gang	Group of Workers
Counseling Group	Music Group
Volunteer Group	Military

2. Can you add any groups to this list? Write them below.

3. Now think about one of your favorite communities. Answer these questions about that group.

   a. What is the community?

   b. How did you join the community?

   c. How does being part of this community make you feel?

   d. What do you gain from being a member of this community?

Benefits of a Community

Being part of a community has many benefits. First, the community fulfills your need to belong. You connect with others in the community. You feel as if you have something in common with those around you.

This connection makes you feel good. It helps to keep your self-esteem high. Being part of a community makes you feel valuable. It makes you feel special. Belonging to a community helps you have a good opinion of yourself.

Being part of a group also gives you a feeling of safety. You feel as though there are people that you can trust. You feel as if you can depend on these people. They are your friends. They will help keep you safe.

Right now, Carol shows signs of low self-esteem. Why? She doesn't feel as if she belongs. Carol needs to join a new group. It will give her a feeling of acceptance. It will make her feel honored. This will raise her self-esteem.

Check What You've Learned

Read each statement. If the statement is true, write T on the answer blank. If the statement is false, write F on the answer blank. (Check your answers on page 118.)

_____ 1. Members of a community have nothing in common.

_____ 2. Belonging to a community keeps your self-esteem high.

_____ 3. Most people like to be alone.

_____ 4. Only adults belong to communities.

_____ 5. Being part of a group makes a person feel safe.

Finding the Right Group

Carol Domenici decided that she wanted to join a new group. But she didn't know how to find a group she would like. She wanted to make sure that she would have something in common with the other members. Carol didn't want to go someplace where she wouldn't fit in. That would make her feel even worse! That would make her self-esteem even lower!

What About You?

Think about a community you have belonged to which did *not* make you feel good about yourself. Answer these questions about that experience.

1. What was the community?

2. What did the members have in common?

3. Did you have anything in common with the other members? Explain your answer.

4. Why did you join the group in the first place?

5. What effect did belonging to the group have on your self-esteem? Explain your answer.

Steps for Finding the Right Community

There are some things Carol can do to find the community that is right for her. You can follow these steps to find a community that is suited for you!

Step 1: Know Your Values and Goals

The first thing you must do is think about your values and goals. Make a list of the things that are important to you. Write your goals under each value you list. Then look for a community that shares the same values. Try to find a community that has goals similar to yours.

For example, you might value being kind to others. Your goal might be to spend some time helping young children. Using this information as a guide, you could look for a volunteer group that aids children. A child care center, local recreation program, or Big Brother/Big Sister group would be good communities for you to find out about.

Think About It

Read about each person. List the groups each person could join. (Check your answers on page 118.)

1. Larry values living a healthy life. A goal of his is to spend more time working out. Larry would like to join a new community. Name some communities you think Larry should join.

2. Maddie values being a good parent. A goal of hers is to be more active in her children's lives. Maddie would like to join a new community. Name some communities you think Maddie should join.

3. Roberto values living a healthy life. A goal of his is to stop smoking. Roberto would like to join a new community. Name some communities you think Roberto should join.

Step 2: Learn About Groups in Your Area

Your next step in finding a positive community is to learn about the groups in your area. Churches, schools, town halls, and libraries are sources of information about the groups in your area. Many local libraries have information boards that advertise special groups. The local newspaper may print notices about group activities and meetings. You can even look through your local telephone book to find this information.

What About You?_____

Gather information about two different kinds of groups in your area. Follow the tips given above to get this information. Then complete the chart below.

GROUPS IN MY AREA
Group 1
Name of the Group:
Goals of the Group:
How to Join:
Group 2
Name of the Group:
Goals of the Group:
How to Join:

Step 3: Make a Visit

The last thing you should do in order to find a positive community is visit the group that interests you. Go to one meeting. Keep an open mind. Look around you. Learn who is in charge. Ask for information about the goals of the group.

Then think about how you would feel spending time with the members of this community. Think about how you would feel as part of this group. Would you feel honored and respected? Would you feel as if you fit in?

When you get home, think about what you saw. Think about how you felt. Then make a decision. If the group is right for you, join it. If the goals and values of the group do not match your goals and values, look for a different community.

Think About It

Suppose you visited a local community. You found that the goals of the group matched your own. But you discovered that a former boyfriend or girlfriend was a member of the group. You and this person did not end your relationship on good terms. You don't feel comfortable being around the person. Yet you really liked the community. Would you join? Explain.

Check What You've Learned

Read each statement. If the statement is true, write T on the answer blank. If the statement is false, write F on the answer blank. (Check your answers on page 118.)

_____ 1. You should join communities that have goals similar to yours.

_____ 2. You can find out about local communities by looking through a telephone book.

_____ 3. If you visit an organization once, you have to join it.

Dealing With Peer Pressure

Sometimes you join a community that you know is all wrong for you. Why? You do this because of peer pressure.

Peer pressure is the power your friends have to get you to act in a certain way. Peer pressure is very powerful. It can make you do things you don't want to do. It can make you act in ways you know are wrong.

What makes peer pressure so powerful? Your need to belong is what makes it strong. You want to feel like part of a community. You need to feel that you connect with others. This need is so strong that you might do something you don't believe in just to be part of the group.

What About You?_____

Think about a time when you did something you knew was not right. Answer these questions about that time.

1. What did you do?

2. Who asked you to do it?

3. Why did you do it?

4. How did you feel about doing it?

5. If you had to do it over again, would you still act the same way? Explain.

Fighting Peer Pressure

Peer pressure is a fact of life. Young children must deal with peer pressure in school. Teens face peer pressure from gangs and other groups. Even adults face peer pressure.

There are some things you can do to deal with peer pressure. Always remember that *you* are responsible for your choices. No one can force you to do anything. You have the right to say no. Never let anyone take that right away from you.

When you face peer pressure, you should:

- Think about your values and goals.
- Think about your moral code.
- Think about how going along with the group might affect your life.
- Remember that you have choices.
- Remember that you are responsible for the choices you make.

Then you must make a decision. You must decide whether your need to belong is stronger than your need to be true to yourself. Only you know the answer to this question.

Peer Pressure and Self-Esteem

It is easier to fight peer pressure if your self-esteem is high. If you believe that you are a valuable person, you will honor your thoughts and feelings. You will not let a group of people make decisions for you. You will know that you can just say no.

If your self-esteem is low, you are more affected by peer pressure. If your self-esteem is low, you don't think that you are valuable. You rely on others for feelings of worthiness. Other people can use this against you. They can suggest that you are a good person only if you do what they say.

Think About It

Read about each situation. Think about what you would do. Write your answer to each question in the space provided.

1. You haven't been out in quite a while. An old friend calls you. He asks you to go out. You agree to meet him at a bar. He suggests that you both get "good and drunk." "Let's have a good time together," he says.

   a. What does your friend want you to do?

   b. Does getting drunk fit in with your moral code and values?

   c. What choices do you have?

   d. Who is responsible for the choice you make?

   e. What would you do? Explain why.

2. You go to a friend's party. You soon discover that everyone at the party is doing drugs. Someone offers you some. Your friend tells you, "Loosen up and enjoy life. Have some fun for a change."

   a. What does your friend want you to do?

   b. Does doing drugs fit in with your moral code and values?

   c. What choices do you have?

   d. Who is responsible for the choice you make?

   e. What would you do? Explain.

How to Say No

It is hard to go against your friends. But sometimes it is the best thing to do.

If someone tries to get you to do something you don't want to do, just say no. Don't tell the other person that he or she is wrong. Don't make the person feel bad about his or her choice. This could anger the person. It could put you in a dangerous position.

Instead, simply decline. If your friend asks you why, explain how you feel. Concentrate on telling your friend about *your* feelings. Be firm. Let your friend know that you won't change your mind.

You could even thank your friend for thinking of you. Say "Thanks for the offer, but I'd rather not." This shows your friend that you know he or she was thinking of you, but you don't want to act that way.

Sometimes, you will have to walk away from the situation. Don't argue. Don't fight. Don't give in. Be true to yourself and simply walk away.

Remember the experience the next time your friend approaches you. Try not to let the same thing happen again. Don't put yourself in the same position. This may mean ending your friendship. That's OK. It's better to lose one friend than to lose your respect for yourself!

Think About It

Suppose a friend wants to give you some stolen merchandise for free. You don't want to take it. The act would not fit in with your moral code and values. What should you say to your friend? Write your response in the space provided.

Check What You've Learned

Read each statement. If the statement is true, write **T** on the answer blank. If the statement is false, write **F** on the answer blank. (Check your answers on page 118.)

_____ **1.** Peer pressure is the power used by friends to get you to do something.

_____ **2.** Teens are the only ones who face peer pressure.

_____ **3.** People with high self-esteem give in to peer pressure easily.

_____ **4.** It is always better to give in to peer pressure than to lose a friend.

_____ **5.** Sometimes the only way to deal with peer pressure is to walk away.

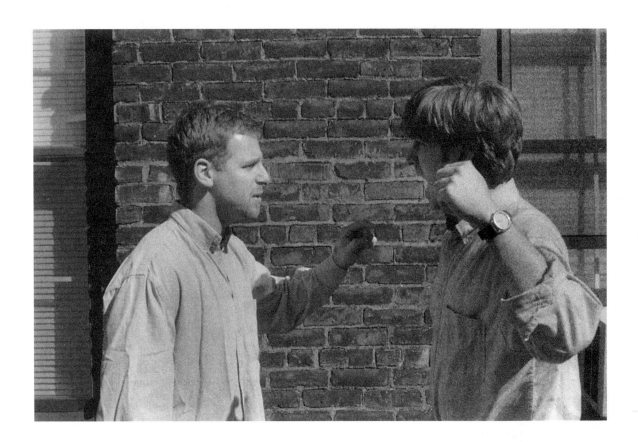

Unit 5 Review

In this unit:

- You discovered that all human beings have a need to belong. Communities are groups of people who have common interests. Communities fulfill the need to belong in a positive way.

- You explored steps in finding positive ways to belong. First you must think about your values and goals. Then you need to find out about groups in your area. You need to match your values and goals with those of a group. It is wise to attend a meeting of a group you are considering joining. This way you can be sure of your decision to join the group.

- You learned that peer pressure is a fact of life. Sometimes, friends will try to get you to do things you don't agree with. Keeping your self-esteem high is one way of dealing with peer pressure. Another way of fighting peer pressure is simply to say no.

Key Words

Use your own words to explain the meaning of each word below. Write your answers below. (Check your answers on page 118.)

1. community

2. peer pressure

Key Ideas

Write the answer to each question in the space provided. (Check your answers on page 118.)

1. Name three communities to which you belong.

2. Give two reasons why people join communities.

3. How can belonging to a community raise your self-esteem?

4. What are the steps one should follow when looking for a group to join?

5. How does high self-esteem help you fight peer pressure?

6. What are some things you should think of when facing peer pressure to do something that you believe is wrong?

7. Is it better to give in to peer pressure than to lose a friend? Explain.

What About You? _____

What was the most important thing you learned in Unit 5? How can you use this information in your daily life?

Respect Differences

In this unit you will:

- discover that making unfair judgments is harmful.
- learn how to show respect for the differences between people.

Key Words

discrimination: denying some people the rights and benefits that others have
respect: to honor another

Meet Quentin Davis

Quentin Davis owns a local market. He knows most of his customers very well. They live in the neighborhood. They shop in his store often.

One afternoon, a middle-aged woman came into Quentin's store. Quentin looked at the woman closely. He had never seen her before. She looked very ordinary. She wore pair of black pants and a sweater. She carried a large purse. Quentin nodded hello as she passed. Then he went back to stocking the shelves.

The woman roamed around the store. No one paid any attention to her. No one noticed that she put some things in her large bag. No one noticed that she only paid for a small box of cereal.

Soon after the woman left, another customer came into the store. He was a young male. Quentin looked at him closely. He had never seen the man before.

"Boy, there's a strange one," Quentin thought to himself. The man was dressed all in black. He wore shiny red boots. Many gold chains sparkled around his neck.

What Quentin noticed the most was the man's hair. It was dyed three different colors. Strands of blue, red, and green were mixed together.

Quentin had never seen hair like that before.

Think About It _____

Circle the letter of the statement that best completes the sentence. (Check your answer on page 118.)

Quentin did not know that the woman
    a. had just moved into the neighborhood.
    b. did not have any money.
    c. stole things and put them in her bag.
    d. was a police officer.

Discrimination

Quentin Davis frowned as the man passed him. Then he noticed that the man carried a large backpack. "Hey," Quentin called to the man. "You'll have to leave that here."

"What?" asked the man. He walked toward Quentin. "I'm sorry. I didn't hear you. What did you say?" he asked.

"Store policy," Quentin responded. "All customers have to leave their bags by the register." He pointed toward the man's backpack. "You'll have to leave that with me."

The man thought for a moment. "OK," he said. He gave Quentin the backpack. Then he began to shop.

Quentin kept a close eye on the man. He used the store mirrors to watch what the man did. The man simply shopped as Quentin watched.

Finally, the man was ready to pay for his things. Quentin rang up the purchases. He told the man how much he owed. The man reached into his backpack. He handed Quentin a hundred-dollar bill.

"I can't take this," Quentin said angrily. He wasn't going to take any chances with this guy. How could he be sure that the money was real?

"Why not?" the man asked.

"I don't have enough change," Quentin lied.

The man looked out the store window. He saw a bank across the street. "Just a minute, please. I'll run across the street and get some smaller bills."

Quentin stood by the register. He watched the man walk into the bank. In a few minutes the man reappeared. He came back to Quentin's store and handed Quentin a twenty.

Quentin counted out the man's change. He roughly slapped the money on the counter. "Thanks," the man replied. He picked up his bags and left the store.

Quentin sighed. Then he went back to stocking the shelves.

Think About It

Circle the letter of the statement that best completes each sentence. (Check your answers on page 118.)

1. Quentin told the man he had to
   a. leave the store.
   b. pay with a hundred-dollar bill.
   c. leave his backpack by the register.
   d. take his business elsewhere.

2. As the man shopped, Quentin
   a. called the police.
   b. took his picture.
   c. went back to stocking the shelves.
   d. watched him in the store mirrors.

3. Quentin thought that the man might
   a. give him fake money.
   b. give him a tip.
   c. rob the bank.
   d. take the woman's purse.

The Harm in Unfair Judgments

Quentin treated the man and the woman quite differently. Why? He made unfair judgments about them. He based his judgments on the way they looked.

When Quentin looked at the woman, he saw someone who looked ordinary. She dressed the same way that many of his customers dressed. Quentin used his observations of her appearance to make a judgment. He judged the woman to be safe. He didn't worry about her. He didn't think that she would steal from him. So, he didn't tell her that she had to leave her large purse by the register. He didn't bother to watch her. He went back to stocking the shelves.

Quentin's judgment was very wrong. The woman *did* steal from him. She might have looked the same as many of his customers. But she acted in a very different manner.

Quentin also judged the man according to his appearance. The man was dressed differently. His hairstyle was different. Quentin saw these differences as

87

bad. He judged the man based on his differences. Quentin judged the man to be dangerous.

Quentin thought that the man might steal from him. So he made the man leave his backpack by the register. Quentin thought that the man might be using fake money. So he refused to take a large bill from the man.

Once again, Quentin's judgment was very wrong. The man was not trying to rob him. The man was not using fake money. The man was an ordinary customer. He might have looked different. But he behaved in the same way as Quentin's other customers.

Quentin's actions showed discrimination. **Discrimination** is showing favoritism based on a difference. Quentin treated his two new customers in different ways. His discrimination was based upon the way they looked.

Quentin's discrimination hurt two people that day. It hurt the man. He was not treated fairly. He was misjudged because of his different appearance.

Quentin's discrimination also hurt Quentin. How? He lost money when the woman stole from him. But Quentin has only himself to blame. He should have treated both new customers the same way. He should have asked the woman to leave her large purse by the register. He should have watched her the way he watched the man. If he hadn't discriminated, or showed favoritism, she wouldn't have been able to steal from him.

What About You?

Think about a time when you were treated differently because of your appearance. Answer these questions about that experience.

1. Where were you?

2. How were you treated?

3. Why were you treated that way?

4. How did the discrimination make you feel?

Making Unfair Judgments

People often make judgments based on what they see. But when you treat a person unfairly because of such a judgment, you are discriminating.

Discriminating is harmful. It hurts the other person. It also hurts you. It can keep you from meeting someone with whom you could be good friends. It can keep you from learning new things. It can prevent you from meeting your true partner.

Think About It

Read the description of each person. Answer the questions that follow.

1. A friend wants you to go out with someone. He shows you a picture of the person. The person is dressed in a tight gray suit. The person has very short, straight hair. The person is wearing thick black glasses.

   What would you think if you saw this photo? Would you go out with the person? Explain.

2. You need to leave your toddler with a baby-sitter. Your regular sitter is unavailable. A friend says that you can use her sitter. You have never met this girl. Five minutes before you are to leave, the doorbell rings. You open the door to find a teenager who looks as old as you do. She is wearing a very short skirt and a tight blouse. Her hair is piled high on top of her head. She is wearing a lot of makeup and false eyelashes.

   What would you think as you looked at this baby-sitter? Would you leave your toddler with her? Explain.

Treat Others Fairly

When you meet someone, you use your senses to gather information about the person. How the person looks, what the person says, how the person acts—all provide you with clues about the person.

However, you must be careful not to use these clues to make a quick judgment. You could be very wrong about the person.

Don't think about the way the person differs from you. Instead, think about the ways that you are alike. This will give you a link to the person. It will open up new lines of communication. It will give you more information about the individual.

Treating a person fairly shows that you respect the individual. **Respect** means that you honor the person. Respect means that you will not judge the person unfairly.

Your words and actions will send a message to the other person. They say, "I accept you." The other person will hear this message and will treat you the same way. You will hear the same message. You will feel good about yourself. Your self-esteem will grow.

Check What You've Learned

Read each statement. If the statement is true, write T on the answer blank. If the statement is false, write F on the answer blank. (Check your answers on page 118.)

_____ 1. Discrimination means treating all people the same.

_____ 2. When you discriminate, you hurt yourself.

_____ 3. Discrimination can stop you from making new friends.

_____ 4. When you respect someone else, you honor that person.

_____ 5. Treating others fairly can help raise your self-esteem.

Show Respect for Others

You are different from every other human being. No one looks exactly the same as you do. No one thinks exactly the same as you do. No one lives the exact same life as you do.

There are many reasons you are different from others. You received a set of traits, or characteristics, from your parents. These traits determined many parts of you. Your hair color, eye color, height, and weight are some characteristics you received from your parents.

Another reason you are different is your background. You grew up in a certain place. Your family is made up of certain people. You did certain things. No one else grew up in exactly the same way you did.

Your values, goals, and moral code make you different from others. You have certain ideas about what is right and what is wrong. Particular things are important to you. There are certain things that you hope to achieve.

Your everyday life experiences also make you different. No one else lives exactly like you do. No one else has exactly the same interests, hobbies, job, friends, or problems. No one is exactly like you.

What About You?

You probably think that you and a good friend or partner are very much alike. In this activity, you will discover just how different you are.

Read the questions on the next page. On the left side of the page, write *your* answer to each one. Then ask a close friend or partner the same questions. Write this person's answers on the right side of the page.

1. Where were you born?

Me   **Friend or Partner**

2. How many people were in your family?

Me   **Friend or Partner**

3. Where did you attend grade school?

Me   **Friend or Partner**

4. What is your favorite color?

Me   **Friend or Partner**

5. How tall are you?

Me   **Friend or Partner**

6. What do you like to do in your spare time?

Me   **Friend or Partner**

7. What is your favorite food?

Me   **Friend or Partner**

8. If you could have any job, what would it be?

Me   **Friend or Partner**

Now go back and circle all the questions to which you and your friend or partner gave the same answer. Are more questions circled or uncircled? Are you and your friend or partner more alike or different? Explain your answer.

How to Show Respect

When you meet others, you want to be accepted. You want to be judged fairly. You don't want others to discriminate against you. You don't want them to see only the way you differ from them.

Other people want you to treat them the same way. They want to be treated with respect. There are some things that you can do to make sure that you show respect for others.

- **Look at Others' Strengths**
  When you meet someone for the first time, don't think about how the person looks. Rather, think about how the person is special. Get to know the person's strengths.

- **Learn About Others**
  Make an effort to learn about people who are different from you. It is all right to ask questions. This will help you gain information. It will help you come to understand others. By asking questions, you show others that you value them. Your questions show that you believe that they are important.

- ## Be Aware of Your Actions
  Think about how you act around people who are different. Do you treat them fairly? Think about why you act this way. Then take some steps to try to change your behavior.

- ## Teach Others
  Unfair treatment happens when people do not understand each other. You can help prevent this by telling others about the communities to which you belong. Let others know the goals of your communities. Explain to others why your communities do certain things. Teach people about yourself.

- ## Speak Respectfully
  The way you speak to a person shows whether or not you respect that individual. When possible, use the person's name. Look at the person's face as you speak. If the person responds, listen carefully. Never yell or shout at someone.

What About You?

Think about a time when someone did *not* treat you in a respectful manner. Answer these questions about that experience.

1. What did the person say that showed that you were not respected?

2. What did the person do that showed that you were not respected?

3. How did the person's words and actions make you feel?

4. What did *you* do?

Check What You've Learned

Read each statement. If the statement is true, write T on the answer blank. If the statement is false, write F on the answer blank. (Check your answers on page 118.)

_____ 1. All people have the same traits.

_____ 2. Your background makes you unique or special.

_____ 3. All people want to be judged fairly.

_____ 4. Walking away from a person who is talking to you shows the person that he is valued.

_____ 5. Teaching people about you and the communities to which you belong is one way to stop discrimination.

Unit 6 Review

In this unit:

- You discovered that making unfair judgments harms both you and the person you are judging. It leads to discrimination. Instead, you should respect others and let them know they are valuable.

- You learned that no two people are exactly alike. Each person is unique. You can show that you respect others by looking for their strengths, learning about people who are different from you, being aware of your actions, teaching others about yourself, and speaking in a respectful manner.

Key Words

Use your own words to explain the meaning of each term listed below. (Check your answers on page 118.)

1. discrimination

2. respect

Key Ideas

Write the answer to each question in the space provided. (Check your answers on page 119.)

1. Is discrimination helpful or harmful? Explain why.

2. When meeting a new person, should you think about the way you are alike or about the way you are different? Explain.

3. What effect does treating a person with respect have on your self-esteem?

4. Name four ways people are different.

5. Name four ways to show respect for others.

6. How can teaching others about yourself help stop discrimination?

What About You? _____

What was the most important thing you learned in Unit 6? How can you use this information in your daily life?

Put It Into Practice

In this unit you will:

- review the key ideas of this book.
- show that you understand the need for values and goals.
- practice what you have learned.

Be Proud of Yourself

You have just learned a great deal by working through this book. You thought about your own moral code, values, and goals. You learned how to set good goals for yourself. You discovered positive ways of belonging. You learned why people are different. You explored ways of showing respect for others.

Working through this book taught you many new skills. You can use these skills every day of your life. They will help you achieve the things you want. They will help you treat others fairly.

In this unit, you will practice the skills you have learned. The practice will help make your skills stronger.

Reviewing Unit 1: The Importance of Self-Esteem

In Unit 1 you learned about self-esteem. You discovered that high self-esteem helps you work toward your goals. You explored ways of improving self-esteem.

Think about these things. Look back at Unit 1. Then work through the following activities. They will strengthen the skills you developed in Unit 1.

Think About It

Use your own words to describe self-esteem. Write your answer in the space provided. (Check your answer on page 119.)

Check What You've Learned

Read each statement. If it shows high self-esteem, write H on the answer blank. If it shows low self-esteem, write L on the answer blank. (Check your answers on page 119.)

_____ 1. I know that I am good at certain things.

_____ 2. I'm afraid that I can't do anything right.

_____ 3. Why should I even bother to try? I'll probably just mess everything up.

_____ 4. I wish I were like everyone else.

_____ 5. So what if I made a mistake. I'm human.

_____ 6. I'm going to try to learn how to do this. I'll never know what it's like until I try.

_____ 7. I know that if I work hard enough, I'll be able to get this job done.

_____ 8. I'm no good at anything.

_____ 9. Why would anyone want me around? I'm a loser.

_____ 10. I know that I am valuable.

_____ 11. I'm going to give this thing a try. What do I have to lose?

_____ 12. I really can't stand myself sometimes.

_____ 13. Who would want to go out with me? I'm a wreck.

_____ 14. I'm going to try to be the best person I can.

_____ 15. I think it's time for a change. I want to get rid of some of my bad habits.

Think About It

Write your answers to each question in the space provided. (Check your answers on page 119.)

1. Use your own words to explain what goals are.

2. Explain how high self-esteem helps you reach your goals.

3. Explain how low self-esteem can keep you from reaching your goals.

Reviewing Unit 2: Strengths and Weaknesses

In Unit 2 you learned that being positive can help build self-esteem. You thought about your strengths and weaknesses. You practiced turning weaknesses into strengths.

Think about these things. Look back at Unit 2. Then work through the following activities. They will strengthen the skills you developed in Unit 2.

Think About It

Use your own words to describe "being positive." (Check your answer on page 119.)

Check What You've Learned

Look at each trait listed below. If the trait is a strength, write S on the answer blank. If the trait is a weakness, write W on the answer blank. (Check your answers on page 119.)

_____ Friendly

_____ Bored

_____ Artistic

_____ Creative

_____ Spends too much

_____ Loses temper easily

_____ Likes to help others

_____ Lazy

_____ Drinks too much

_____ Athletic

_____ Shy

_____ Likes to save

_____ Patient

_____ Untrustworthy

Think About It

Write your answer to each question in the space provided. (Check your answers on page 119.)

1. How does using your strengths help keep your self-esteem high?

2. How does being positive help boost self-esteem?

What About You?

1. Name three of your strengths.

2. Name three of your weaknesses.

3. Think about how you could turn one of the weaknesses you just named into a strength.

4. How would this make you feel about yourself?

Reviewing Unit 3: Values

In Unit 3 you thought about your moral code. You became aware of your goals and values. You discovered how to set good goals for yourself.

Think about these things. Look back at Unit 3. Then work through the following activities. They will strengthen the skills you developed in Unit 3.

Think About It

Write your answer to each question in the space provided. (Check your answers on page 119.)

1. Use your own words to describe a moral code.

2. Name five things that affect your moral code.

What About You?

Write your answer to each question in the space provided.

1. Suppose a friend asked you to hide some stolen goods for him. How would thinking about your values help you decide what to do?

2. What would you tell your friend? Explain.

Think About It

Write a letter to a friend explaining how goals and values are connected.

Dear _____,

What About You?

1. Think about one of your most important values. Write it in the space provided.

2. Name three goals that match this value.

Goal 1:

Goal 2:

Goal 3:

3. Look at the three goals you listed above. Think about the traits of a good goal. Are these goals good? Explain why or why not.

Goal 1:

Goal 2:

Goal 3:

Reviewing Unit 4: Goals

In Unit 4 you learned more about making reasonable goals. You practiced making personal goals that are good for you. You discovered that making a plan and schedule help you to achieve your goals.

Think about these things. Look back at Unit 4. Then work through the following activities. They will strengthen the skills you developed in Unit 4.

Think About It _____

Use your own words to describe the traits of a reasonable goal. (Check your answer on page 119.)

Check What You've Learned

Listed below are different goals. Read each one. If the goal is reasonable, put a **+** on the answer blank. If the goal is not reasonable, put a **-** on the answer blank. (Check your answers on page 119.)

_____ 1. During the next six months, I want to learn to drive.

_____ 2. I want to quit smoking today.

_____ 3. I want to start exercising. I'll begin by walking for 15 minutes every day.

_____ 4. I want to learn how to speak Spanish. I'll sign upfor a course in beginning Spanish at the local school.

_____ 5. I need to change my wardrobe. I'm going to get rid of all my old clothes. Then I'll buy new things that are totally different.

_____ 6. By the end of this week I will lose 10 pounds.

_____ 7. I'm going to start a new life. I will move, find a new job, and make new friends before next Saturday.

_____ 8. I want to clean my entire apartment. I'll start now and won't stop until everything is done.

_____ 9. I want to save some money. I'll save at least $10 every week.

_____ 10. I want to stop drinking. I'm going to cut back a little bit each day. By next month, I should be off alcohol.

Think About It

Write your answers to each question in the space provided. (Check your answers on page 119.)

1. Look back at the goals you marked with a **-** in the previous activity. Rewrite the goals to make them more reasonable.

2. Explain how making a plan and keeping to a schedule help you reach your goals.

What about You? _____

Name a personal goal of yours. Then make a plan for accomplishing your goal. Be sure that your plan contains a series of small steps that are linked.

My Goal:

My Plan:

Think About It _____

Suppose a friend told you that he or she wanted to lose 10 pounds. Write your friend a letter explaining what he or she should do to reach this goal.

Dear _____,

Reviewing Unit 5: Belonging

In Unit 5 you discovered that all human beings have a need to belong. You discovered that belonging to communities helps keep your self-esteem high. You explored steps to finding positive ways to belong. You found that peer pressure can cause you to make bad choices.

Think about these things. Look back at Unit 5. Then work through the following activities. They will strengthen the skills you developed in Unit 5.

Think About It

Write your answer to each question in the space provided. (Check your answers on page 119.)

1. Describe one way that you are just like all other people.

2. How does belonging to a community help keep your self-esteem high?

What About You?

Write your answers to each question in the space provided.

1. List all the communities or groups to which you belong.

2. What are the benefits of belonging to these groups?

Think About It

Write the answer to each question in the space provided. (Check your answers on page 119.)

1. Suppose you wanted to find a community to join. What things should you do to find the community that is right for you?

2. Use your own words to describe peer pressure.

3. Can peer pressure ever be a good thing? Explain.

Check What You've Learned

Read the following list of actions. Put a check mark next to those that would help you fight peer pressure. (Check your answers on page 119.)

_____ Think about what your friends want for you.

_____ Think about your moral code.

_____ Forget about your values.

_____ Understand your friends' goals.

_____ Go along with others.

_____ Start an argument.

_____ Remember your personal goals.

_____ Just do what everyone else does.

_____ Blame your actions on someone else.

_____ Think about how your decision will affect your life.

_____ Remember that you should make choices that are good for you.

Reviewing Unit 6: Respect Differences

In Unit 6 you discovered that making unfair judgments harms both you and the person you judge. You saw how unfair judgments can lead to discrimination. You learned ways of showing respect for the differences that exist between people.

Think about these things. Look back at Unit 6. Then work through the following activities. They will strengthen the skills you developed in Unit 6.

Think About It

Write your answer to each question in the space provided. (Check your answers on page 120.)

1. Use your own words to describe an unfair judgment.

2. Use your own words to describe discrimination.

Check What You've Learned

Read each statement. Put a **+** on the answer blank if the statement shows respect for others. Put a **-** on the answer blank if the statement does not show respect for others. (Check your answers on page 120.)

_____ **1.** That's an interesting ring. Does it have a special meaning?

_____ **2.** That's the weirdest hairdo I've ever seen.

_____ **3.** No one I know would wear an outfit like that.

_____ **4.** Watch out for that guy. He looks really strange.

_____ **5.** People who wear clothes like that are trouble.

_____ **6.** How can you eat that food? It looks terrible.

_____ **7.** Even though we seem different, I bet we have some things in common.

_____ **8.** Tell me more about why you are dressed that way.

_____ **9.** That person looks like someone I know. I guess it's safe to be with him.

_____ **10.** We don't go out with people who belong to that group.

_____ **11.** I would never go out with her. She's too weird.

_____ **12.** Your home is very unusual. It's nice to see something different for a change.

_____ **13.** How can you be around that guy? He looks so strange.

_____ **14.** Even though we come from different places, I know we like many of the same things.

_____ **15.** I'd like to learn more about you. Can you explain why you eat that kind of food?

Think About It

How can treating others fairly make the world a better place? Explain. (Check your answer on page 120.)

BOOK REVIEW

Key Words

Match each word in Column A with the correct definition in Column B. Write the letter from Column B on the line. (Check your answers on page 120.)

Column A

_____ **1.** community

_____ **2.** discrimination

_____ **3.** goal

_____ **4.** moral code

_____ **5.** negative

_____ **6.** peer pressure

_____ **7.** plan

_____ **8.** positive

_____ **9.** religion

_____ **10.** respect

_____ **11.** schedule

Column B

a. something you hope to achieve

b. good qualities that you like about yourself

c. a series of steps for accomplishing a goal

d. bad qualities that youdo not like about yourself

e. a time line for getting something done

f. any group that lives in the same place or has common interest

g. things that are important to you

h. to honor another

i. denying some people the rights or benefits that others have

j. a set of rules having to do with right and wrong

k. a system of beliefs or worship

_____ **12.** self-esteem

_____ **13.** strengths

_____ **14.** values

_____ **15.** weaknesses

l. bad; harmful

m. power used by friends to get you to do something or to act in a certain way

n. good; healthy

o. your opinion of yourself

Key Ideas _____

Write the answer to each question in the space provided. (Check your answers on page 120.)

1. What is the difference between high and low self-esteem?

2. How can you change your self-esteem?

3. What effect does being positive have on self-esteem?

4. What things affect your moral code?

5. Explain how goals and values are related.

6. Describe a reasonable goal.

7. How does making a plan and schedule help you reach your goals?

8. What is a community? Give two examples.

9. What are some benefits of belonging to a community?

10. What are some things a person can do to find positive ways to belong?

11. How can peer pressure cause you to make bad choices?

12. How can you fight peer pressure?

13. Explain how unfair judgments and discrimination are related.

14. What can you do to make sure that you treat others fairly?

Book Review

GLOSSARY

community: any group that lives in the same place or has common interests, 70

discrimination: denying some people the rights of benefits that others have, 88

goal: something you hope to achieve, 8

moral code: a set of rules having to do with right and wrong, 37

negative: bad; harmful, 12

peer pressure: power used by friends to get you to do something or to act in a certain way, 77

plan: a series of steps for accomplishing a goal, 56

positive: good; healthy, 11

religion: a system of beliefs or worship, 38

respect: to honor another, 90

schedule: a time line for getting something done, 58

self-esteem: your opinion of yourself, 4

strengths: good qualities that you like about yourself, 23

values: things that are important to you, 40

weaknesses: bad qualities that you do not like about yourself, 24

ANSWER KEY

UNIT 1: The Importance of Self-Esteem

Think About It (p. 2)
1. b   **2.** a

Think About It (p. 4)

c

Check What You've Learned (p. 6)

1. F   **2.** F   **3.** T   **4.** T   **5.** T

Check What You've Learned (p. 10)
1. F   **2.** F   **3.** T   **4.** F   **5.** F

Check What You've Learned (p. 14)
1. F   **2.** F   **3.** T   **4.** T   **5.** T

Unit 1 Review

Key Words (p. 15)
1. c   **2.** d   **3.** a   **4.** b

Key Ideas (pp. 15-16)
1. Self-esteem is your opinion of yourself.
2. They like themselves, feel powerful and strong, and know that they have good and bad traits.
3. They feel hopeless and that everything they do is wrong.
4. Goals are something you hope to achieve.
5. No, because people are different and have different values.
6. High self-esteem gives you a feeling of power. You believe in yourself and in your abilities. You are willing to try to achieve the things you desire.
7. Low self-esteem makes you feel hopeless and believe that there is no point in trying to reach your goals. You'll probably just fail.
8. Think about who you are, name your positive traits, and think about what you'd like to change about yourself and why you'd like the change.

UNIT 2: Strengths and Weaknesses

Think About It (p. 18)
1. c   **2.** d

Think About It (p. 20)
Jack's boss gave Mrs. Rogers a favorable picture of Jack.

Think About It (p. 21)
It is unlikely that Jack would have been hired because Mrs. Rogers would have realized that he lied.

Check What You've Learned (p. 22)
1. F   **2.** F   **3.** T

Think About It (p. 26)
1. Answers may include displaying her art in her home, giving her art to others as gifts, volunteering to work on an outdoor mural in her neighborhood.
2. Answers may include repairing the cars of friends and neighbors, volunteering to work on cars used by charity groups.
3. Answers may include baby-sitting for a neighbor and volunteering to work in a local recreation program.
4. Answers may include reading to an elderly person and volunteering to read to children in a local school or library.

Think About It (p. 27)
1. Answers may include making tapes for the visually impaired and working as a switchboard operator.
2. Answers may include working in a repair shop or helping friends and neighbors fix broken items.
3. Answers may include helping friends or neighbors organize their closets and working for a caterer that prepares food for large parties.

Unit 2 Review

Key Words (p. 28)
1. Good qualities that you like about yourself
2. Bad qualities that you do not like about yourself

Key Ideas (pp. 28–29)
1. A positive person knows that he or she has good points and shows these abilities to others.
2. Strengths are good qualities that you like about yourself, and weaknesses are bad qualities that you do not like about yourself.
3. No. They think about their weaknesses and try to improve themselves.
4. It means make the most of your strengths by finding ways to use them.
5. No. Some are simply bad.

Real-World Connection: The Neat Freak

Key Words (p. 32)
1. c   2. a   3. b   4. d   5. c
6. b   7. a   8. c   9. d   10. a

Check What You've Learned (p. 33)
1. c   2. b   3. a   4. c   5. c
6. b   7. a

Think About It (p. 33)
Carla turned her need for order into a positive skill necessary for the file clerk job.

UNIT 3: Values

Think About It (p. 35)
d

Think About It (p. 37)
1. c   2. b

Check What You've Learned (p. 39)
1. T   2. T   3. T   4. F

Check What You've Learned (p. 42)
1. F   2. T   3. T

Check What You've Learned (p. 45)
1. T   2. F   3. F   4. F   5. T

Unit 3 Review

Key Words (p. 46)
1. b   2. c   3. a

Key Ideas (pp. 46-47)
1. No. Each person is a unique individual.
2. Answers should include family, childhood, friends, religion, laws.
3. Thinking about your values helps you make decisions that are wise for you and that you won't regret later.
4. Yes. Goals should match values.
5. High self-esteem gives you confidence and the power to try to work toward your goals.
6. Low self-esteem makes you feel powerless and unwilling to try and reach your goals.
7. A reasonable goal should match your values, be "doable"
8. Reasonable goals are more likely to be attained than goals that are not reasonable. This success will make you feel good about yourself.

Real-World Connection: The Letter

Key Words (p. 50)
1. c   2. b   3. c   4. d   5. c
6. b   7. a   8. c   9. c

Check What You've Learned (p. 51)
1. c   2. b   3. d   4. a
5. b   6. a   7. c

Think About It (p. 51)
Because Paul and Kit had been taught differently about whether to call parents at work, they disagreed about Paul's action.

UNIT 4: Goals

Think About It (p. 54)
1. c   2. d

Think About It (pp. 55-56)
1. b   2. a
3. Tia has low self-esteem because she has a negative opinion about herself.

Think About It (pp. 58-60)
1. No. The goal is not achievable.
2. No. The daily distance should be less.
3. Yes. The goal is broken down into a series of small, reasonable steps.
4. No. Jon should start off with easier books.
5. No. He should practice before playing with the team.
6. Yes. The goal is broken down into a series of small, reasonable steps.
7. Answers will vary.

Check What You've Learned (p. 61)
1. b   2. a   3. a   4. F
5. T   6. T   7. T   8. T

Unit 4 Review

Key Words (p. 64)
1. A series of steps for accomplishing a goal
2. A time line for getting something done

Key Ideas (p. 65)
1. A reasonable goal matches your values, is achievable, and makes you stretch.
2. A plan breaks down the goal into a series of steps that are connected.
3. A schedule keeps you focused on your goal.

Unit 5: Belonging

Think About It (p. 67)
d

Think About It (p. 69)
1. b   2. a

Check What You've Learned (p. 72)
1. F   2. T   3. F   4. F   5. T

Think About It (pp. 74-75)
1. Answers may include joining a local recreation group, a sports team, or an athletic club.
2. Answers may include joining the local parent–teacher organization and volunteering to be a scout leader.
3. Answers may include joining a local branch of Smoke-Enders or some similar stop-smoking group.

Check What You've Learned (p. 76)
1. T   2. T   3. F

Check What You've Learned (p. 81)
1. T   2. F   3. F   4. F   5. T

Unit 5 Review

Key Words (p. 82)
1. Any group that lives in the same place or has common interests
2. Power used by friends to get you to do something or to act in a certain way

Key Ideas (p. 83)
1. Answers may include a family, sports team, church group, or local club.
2. To fulfill the need to belong; to feel safe
3. Belonging makes you feel valued and accepted.
4. Think about your values and goals; learn about the communities in your area; visit one meeting of the group.
5. High self-esteem helps fight peer pressure because it gives you a feeling of power. You know who you are and what kind of life you want to live.
6. Think about your values and goals; think about your moral code; consider the consequences of your actions; know that you are responsible for your choices
7. No. It is better to honor your own moral code, values, and goals.

UNIT 6: Respect Differences

Think About It (p. 85)
c

Think About It (p. 87)
1. c   2. d   3. a

Check What You've Learned (p. 90)
1. F   2. T   3. T   4. T   5. T

Check What You've Learned (p. 95)
1. F   2. T   3. T   4. F   5. T

Unit 6 Review

Key Words (p. 96)
1. Denying some people the rights or benefits that others have
2. To honor another

Key Ideas (p. 97)

1. Harmful. It hurts you and the person being judged.
2. Alike. Thinking this way opens up lines of communication and helps you get to know the person better.
3. The person returns the respect. This makes you feel valued and honored. Your self-esteem improves.
4. Traits; background; goals, values, and moral code; life experiences
5. Answers should include: look for strengths; learn about those who are different; be aware of your actions; teach others about yourself and the communities you belong to; speak respectfully.
6. By informing others, you help to spread information. This reduces fear of the unknown, which leads to discrimination and unfair judgments.

UNIT 7: Put It Into Practice

Think About It (p. 99)

Self-esteem means that you believe in yourself and your abilities. You are willing to try to reach your goals.

Check What You've Learned (p. 100)

1. H	2. L	3. L	4. L	5. H
6. H	7. H	8. L	9. L	10. H
11. H	12. L	13. L	14. H	
15. H				

Think About It (pp. 100-101)

1. Goals are achievements for which you have to work.
2. When you feel good about yourself, you have the ability to work toward a goal.
3. Low self-esteem makes you think that you will fail.

Think About It (p. 101)

Believing in yourself; knowing that you have certain strengths; knowing that you have the right to live the kind of life you want

Check What You've Learned (p. 102)

Strengths are: friendly, artistic, athletic, creative, likes to save, patient, likes to help others. Weaknesses are: lazy, bored, drinks too much, shy, spends too much, loses temper easily, untrustworthy.

Think About It (p. 102)

1. Others will notice your positive traits and value you. You will feel their respect. This will raise your self-esteem.
2. Having a positive outlook keeps your opinion of yourself high.

Think About It (p. 103)

1. A moral code is a set of beliefs about right and wrong.
2. Rules about what is right and wrong; goals and values; background; religion; laws; and life experiences

Think About It (p. 105)

A reasonable goal fits in with your moral code, matches your values, is achievable, and makes you stretch.

Check What You've Learned (p. 106)

1. +	2. -	3. +	4. +	5. -
6. -	7. -	8. -	9. +	10. -

Think About It (p. 106)

1. Answers will vary.
2. A plan breaks down the goal into a series of steps. It also provides a set of directions about how to achieve the goal. A schedule keeps you focused on the plan. It makes you accountable for doing each step by a certain deadline.

Think About It (p. 108)

1. All human beings have a need to belong. Joining a community fulfills that need.
2. It makes you feel honored and respected.

Think About It (p. 109)

1. Think about your values and goals; learn about local communities; visit one meeting
2. Peer pressure is power used by friends to get you to do something or to act in a certain way.
3. Peer pressure could be positive if the act is something that fits with your goals and values.

Check What You've Learned (p. 109)

Think about your moral code; remember your personal goals; think about how your decision will affect your life; remember to make choices that are good for you.

Think About It (p. 110)

1. An unfair judgment is a quick decision about a person that is not based on all the facts.
2. Discrimination is showing favoritism based on a difference.

Check What You've Learned (pp. 110-111)

1. + 2. - 3. - 4. - 5. -
6. - 7. + 8. + 9. - 10. -
11. - 12. + 13. - 14. + 15. +

Think About It (p. 111)

The world would be a place of mutual respect. Discrimination would stop.

Book Review

Key Words (pp. 112-113)

1. f 2. i 3. a 4. j 5. l
6. m 7. c 8. n 9. k 10. h
11. e 12. o 13. b 14. g 15. d

Key Ideas (pp. 113–114)

1. High self-esteem means that you have a good opinion of yourself. You like yourself. You know that you have strengths and weaknesses. Low self-esteem means that you dislike yourself. You have a low opinion of yourself. You feel as if you do nothing right.
2. Think about your strengths; be positive; work to improve your weaknesses
3. Being positive helps keep self-esteem high.
4. Family; background; religion; laws; life experiences
5. Values are things that you feel are important. Goals are the things you hope to achieve. Your goals and values should match.
6. Fits your values and moral code; makes you stretch; is achievable.
7. A plan breaks down the goal into steps. A schedule keeps you focused on your plan.
8. Any group that lives in the same place or has common interests; examples will vary.
9. Fulfills your need to belong; makes you feel valued; makes you feel safe
10. Think about goals and values; learn about local communities; visit a meeting
11. Peer pressure can cause you to do things you know are bad just to please others.
12. Think about your moral code, goals, and values; know that you have choices; take responsibility for your decisions; think about the consequences
13. When you make unfair judgments, you reach a conclusion before knowing all the facts. The judgments lead to discrimination, or showing favoritism based upon a difference.
14. Look for strengths; learn about others; teach others about yourself; speak respectfully; think about your actions

PHOTO CREDITS

Page 1   Michael Newman, Photo Edit

Page 10   Michael Newman, Photo Edit

Page 14   Robert Brenner, Photo Edit

Page 17   Jonathan Nourok, Photo Edit

Page 22   Scott and Gillian Aldrich

Page 29   Radi Nabulsi

Page 34   Tony Freeman, Photo Edit

Page 41   Tom McCarthy, Photo Edit

Page 52   Elena Rooraid, Photo Edit

Page 54   Beryl Goldberg

Page 64   Radi Nabulsi

Page 66   Scott and Gillian Aldrich

Page 70   Myrleen Ferguson Cate, Photo Edit

Page 81   Scott and Gillian Aldrich

Page 84   Steve and Mary Beran Skjold

Page 93   Tom McCarthy, Photo Edit

Page 95   Dezso Szuri, The Miami Herald

Page 98   Michael Newman, Photo Edit